Previous Titles from the World of Froud™

Good Faeries / Bad Faeries by Brian Froud: edited by Terri Windling

A Midsummer Night's Faery Tale by Wendy Froud and Terri Windling

Lady Cottington's Pressed Fairies™

Lady Cottington's Pressed Fairy Book by Brian Froud and Terry Jones

Lady Cottington's Pressed Fairy Journal by Brian Froud and Terry Jones

Strange Stains and Mysterious Smells by Brian Froud and Terry Jones

Faeries by Brian Froud and Alan Lee

The Goblin Companion by Brian Froud and Terry Jones

Are All the Giants Dead? by Mary Norton and Brian Froud

The Faeries' Oracle

BRIAN FROUD

Text by
JESSICA MACBETH

Under the supervision and direction of the *faeries*,
especially **Brian's** inspiration faery, **Penelope**,
and **Jessica's** friends **Lyset, Miccon,** *and* **Elspeth,**
with special credit to the **Fee-Lion**

Simon & Schuster
New York   London   Toronto   Sydney   Singapore

SIMON & SCHUSTER
Rockefeller Center
1230 Avenue of the Americas
New York, NY 10020

World of Froud is a trademark of Brian Froud

SIMON & SCHUSTER and colophon are registered trademarks
of Simon & Schuster, Inc.

For information regarding special discounts for bulk
purchases, please contact Simon & Schuster Special Sales
at 1-800-456-6798 or business@simonandschuster.com

Designed by Olga Kaljakin, Aspect Ratio Design

A World of Froud/IMAGINOSIS Production

Manufactured in China

20 19 18 17 16 15 14 13 12 11

Library of Congress Cataloging-in-Publication Data is available upon request

ISBN 0-7432-0111-6

Acknowledgments

Both of us would like to give many thanks to Robert Gould, who has put a great deal of creative energy into bringing this project to fruition. And Muriel Nellis deserves much credit for moving the immovable, and doing her best, which is very good indeed.

From Brian . . .
    To Wendy and Toby Froud with much love and gratitude.

From Jesa . . .
    To the members of the Faery Oracle gang, an Internet writer's critique group formed especially for this book—Eileen Inge Herzberg, Pat MacKenzie, Jonathan MacLane, Nadine MacLane, Nanc' Nelson, Michael Slaughter, Richard Wentk, and Kathy Seven Williams. Without them this book would be much less than it is. It would also have been much less fun to write.
    To Linda Anderson, Linda Causey, Judy Dean, Angela Enthoven, Brian Froud, Robert Gould, Vincent and Leslie Hennigan, Denise Logan, Nanc' Nelson, Beryl Peters, Cherry Trippe, Richard Wentk, Dennis Williams, and Warren Wise, who kept me afloat financially and in other tangible ways while I wrote the book.
    To Ebony Angel, Nancy Hendrickson, Diana Cook, David Cortner, Kim Lewis, Kenny Yapkowitz, Tim Rowe, Phyllis Gottshall, Peggy Webber, Debbie Jones, and a big bunch of other people who have shared ideas, comments, suggestions, and personal wisdom. Not all are directly quoted in the book, but all contributed to the process.
    I especially want to say how much I've enjoyed working with Brian and the faeries. Brian has a generous, caring heart, which shows in his paintings and his personal relationships. I'm tickled pink with polka dots that he chose me to help create *The Faeries' Oracle*. And, of course, the faeries themselves—well, they are always fun.
    May the faeries bless them one and all and fill their paths with joyful surprises. And yours, too, dear reader.

Dedicated to...

Why, to Them, of course!

*"Our frontiers are made of mists and dreams and tender waters:
thresholds are crossed from time to time."*

—Pat O'Shea, *The Hounds of the Morrigan*

"All things absurd, nonlinear, nonsensical, irrational, and madly poetic reveal the secrets of the unconscious and the secret language of Faery."—Brian

CONTENTS

Foreword

Once upon a time I wanted to create a divination deck, and so, like the Fool, I stepped off the cliff into the unknown and started to paint. Weeks later, after much research, I had finished my first card. Looking at the image, I realized what a long and extraordinary journey I had begun. At this rate, it would be a lifetime before I could complete all the paintings, and I was impatient. I wanted to hold the deck in my hands—*now*. So, I thought, why not include every image I paint now in a future deck, and allow the faeries themselves to mold its form and direction?

Over the next ten years I continued to explore Faeryland, drawing and painting what I felt and saw there. The result was a book called *Good Faeries/Bad Faeries*. In that volume the faeries gave tantalizing glimpses into their world and provided clues for humans who would like to communicate with them. This connection with the faeries is wonderful because it gives us an opportunity to experience the world in an open and connected way. But I knew that the images in the book and the promise of communication with the faeries held an even more profound secret. In my dealings with the faeries I had discovered much sense in their seeming nonsense—and I had found that there is great wisdom to be gained if we allow them to turn our prejudices and preconceptions upside down. Now was the time to focus the innate energy of the images toward the oracle deck I had longed for and to discover the deep meaning of the art and the faeries.

The process of creating *The Faeries' Oracle* has been a long and immensely rewarding one filled with extraordinary surprises, courtesy of the faeries. As I found, one of the most treasured gifts they can ever give is of bright inspiration. It was a bright day indeed when I thought to ask my friend Jessica Macbeth to help me listen to wise faery voices. Jessica is a "faerynaut" of extraordinary powers, exploring the deep inner spaces of Faeryland, mapping and recording so we can all follow safely. *The Faeries' Oracle* cards are portals that allow light direct from the faery realms to illuminate our darkness. They reveal a world of connection, meaning, and healing energy. Through these cards we can all be fellow travelers in these magical realms. Welcome to the fellowship of Faery.

Brian Froud

Introduction

Welcome! So pleased to meet you. Those folk over there, flickering on the edge of visibility, are various faeries, and the quiet fellow whose words you read on the preceding page is, of course, Brian Froud, who is a delightful person living at the boundary between Faery and this world. He acts as an ambassador between the worlds through his brilliant art. You'll be hearing from other people later on as well—Nadine, Eileen, Pat, and others. These are people who worked with the cards, listened to the faeries, and helped me to create a better book for you. In a way, dear reader, their voices are surrogate voices for yours. As Brian often says, "Faeries are inclusive, not exclusive." He suggests that you consider what these people have said and think about whether or not it rings true for you. You can use their thoughts as springboards for your own thoughts. They are there to help you focus, which is part of the illumination process. They remind you of the dialogue between the faeries and yourself and that the faeries' messages for you may be different from their messages for others. And, of course, you'll get to know me, Jesa.

I hope you'll enjoy our journey together into the wide, wild, and wonderful otherworld of Faery.

I had intended to stop this introduction right here, but it has been pointed out to me that there is a bit more you may want to know before we go much further.

First, what is "faery"? Is it just that I can't spell? I can't, but I have a spelling checker, so that is not my reason for spelling the word like that. "Faery" is an old term that embraces all the elves and gnomes and fairies and other folk, small and large, of the otherworld. It includes the angels whose wings spread across the cosmos, and the wee things that go bump in the night while they scrub your kitchen, tie your shoes neatly to each other, and knot elf locks in your hair as you sleep.

The word *faery* also means the place—Faery, the land of all the faeries, also known as the otherworld. Faery is alongside our everyday world, almost but not quite in synchronization with us, overlapping in some ways, different in others, and operating on a different level of energy. One of the things I hope you will discover during our journeys into the other-world is how to live in both worlds at once. It is just a matter of learning to increase your range of perceptions, which is much easier than you might expect.

Using the Faeries' Oracle is not like reading any other card deck, whether tarot or oracle. In other decks we (you and I, gentle reader) are working with archetypes and intellectual concepts. In *The Faeries' Oracle* we are, of course, still concerned with those. However, we are also interacting with the living, breathing faery beings. They are just as real as we are, if not more so, but they are very different from us. These differences and the faeries' inimitable approach to life will provide us with some interesting joys, challenges, and experiences as we become acquainted with and use this deck. (Imagine me here with a very wry grin.)

Last, you may be wondering if you really belong on this journey to Faery. You might have bought these cards because they are so beautiful, and now perhaps you are wondering if you really can communicate with the faeries and use the cards "properly." Yes, you most certainly can, although it may take a certain amount of practice-as-a-game. I assure you that you will love the results.

Using the Faeries' Oracle is a lot more fun than you might expect—even if you are expecting a lot of fun. And if you are interested in joining us on the Internet to learn and develop your Faeries' Oracle skills even more, please be sure to read the pages in the back of the book on Recommended Sources.

May the faeries be with you!

Jesa Macbeth

Part One
Faeries and Oracles

How to make friends, influence angels, and read oracles

First Steps into the Otherworld

The first thing I always tell my students about oracles and tarot decks is: *Don't read the book.*

This book, of course, is different. . . .

This book is about the living oracle of the faeries—a set of cards and a way of seeing that is different from standard human tarot and oracle cards. Brian once began to paint a human tarot with faery in it, but that wasn't what the faeries wanted him to do. They wanted him to make their own oracle cards, as nearly as he could without being able to paint in light instead of pigments.

This book is also about a different, intuitive way of reading the cards. It starts by helping you to discover your own meanings and insights in the cards instead of telling you mine. Later on, in Part Two, I'll give you the "starter" interpretations as I (and a few others) see them, but right now you need to be aware that any oracle has many possible valid interpretations. These "meanings" change from moment to moment and person to person. Like the faeries, the definitions are changeable and mutable, depending on how you see the world just now and on what the faeries would like to communicate to you. Here we will focus on discovering your own individual interpretations and your special pathways and connections with the Faeries' Oracle.

So, what I really meant when I told my classes not to read their books was: *Don't read someone else's definitions of the cards until you already have some idea of what they mean to you.*

Discovering what the cards mean to you, actually looking closely enough at them to begin to find some of the faery secrets they hold, will give you a completely different and far more magical and intuitive approach to reading the oracle than memorizing a bunch of definitions. To help you to find your own insights, let's start here with some of the things that you will find useful to do and to understand before you read the second part of this book.

First, take a good look at your attitude. Are you really serious about this? Do you believe you will need to work hard with the cards?

If so, please, don't be like that. As much as you can, let yourself approach the cards and the faeries with a light and playful heart. Consider lightheartedness. We usually think of it as the opposite of having a heavy, sad heart, but the faeries also see it in terms of illumination. A light heart is not only *not* heavy—it is glowing with joyful light. It allows us to see things in a different light. Be prepared to have fun with this. Be ready to enjoy the inevitable faery jokes and games. This lightheartedness will illuminate the Oracle for you, making your insights brighter, the concepts embodied in the cards more luminous, and your heart capable of holding even more light.

Now, with a healthy, playful mind-set, take the deck of cards and randomly spread them out, faces up, on a table—or on the floor if, like me, you prefer a lot of space for working. The first thing you will notice, if you have any experience with tarot or oracle cards at all, is that this is not like any other deck. Well, it wouldn't be, would it? This is a *faery* oracle, and as unique, unpredictable, humorous, profound, and beautiful as you would expect something of Faery to be.

You will also notice that there are different types of pictures, and I'd like you to begin by dividing the cards into groups that seem to go together. Set your own criteria for selecting them and begin to notice how the different images and beings shown on the cards might relate to each other.

For example, you may sort into one group the cards that look rather abstract, while the other cards form a group showing scenes and beings that appear more detailed and realistic. As you try to divide the cards into these two subsets, you will find that there are a few that don't quite fit neatly into either but have qualities of both. They form a third set of their own.

Another way of sorting the cards is to divide them into a set that only shows one individual on the card, and a set that shows two, and another set that shows three or more. Or you can divide them into the faeries who look beautiful, the ones who look funny or amusing, and the ones who may appear menacing or threatening to you.

You might sort them by the what is on the heads of the principle faery in each card. Some wear wreaths of flowers or leaves. Some wear floating crowns of stars. There are woodland-style acorn caps, salmon hats, and many others. There are even the bareheaded faeries. What, if anything, do the members of each of these groups have in common? Can you find a kinship between them?

Use your imagination and intelligence and find a variety of ways to compare and relate and differentiate between the cards. There is no right way or wrong way to do this. It is just practice in looking at the cards and seeing the similarities and differences between them. Be inventive and creative and playful about it. The more you do this, the better you will begin to understand this Oracle and Faery itself.

I hope that you are already doing this and not just reading my words. Very shortly we are going to be discussing things that won't make nearly as much sense if you have not done these preliminary steps.

Please practice this for a while, before you go on.

Next, please pick a card up and look at the back of it. What do you see? Lovely, isn't it? But please remember what you are really looking at. Paper. Colored ink. The card in your hand was made by machines from mundane materials. No magic here, is there? Yet somewhere there is magic in the process of reading an oracle. Where can it be?

All right, turn over the card and look at the face of it. An astonishing work of art, isn't it? But the card, picture and all, is still just ink on a piece of paper. No magic here either, is there? Where is that magic then? If you look at the edge, you will not find a thin layer of something glimmery and glittery sandwiched between the front and the back, so there is probably no magic hidden within the card either. Where can it be if it is not in the cards themselves?

Brace yourself for this.

The magic is in *you*. Many people in this modern, unenlightened age have a hard time believing in faeries, but far more people find it impossible to believe that there is magic in themselves. They can only believe in magic outside of themselves—crystals, incense, drugs, cards, other people, widgets, gizmos, whatever.

Some people can believe in anything—except in themselves. I don't want you to believe in just anything and everything, and I don't want you to believe in anything just because I say it is true. I want you to discover what is *really there*—and you will. But a good place to start is by admitting to yourself that the cards themselves are not magical. The magic of the Oracle, if anywhere (and it is definitely somewhere), is elsewhere.

Not only is this magic in you, but it is also in Faery, it is in Brian and his paintings, and even in me.

You can't miss it.

Okay, now we'll stop fooling around and get down to some serious playing.

Please put that first card back down. Look at the rest of the cards for a while. Take your time looking the cards over and as you look, try to find two special cards: the one that appeals to you the most and the one that appeals to you the least, which makes you the most uncomfortable when you look at it. You may choose several before you settle on the two special ones, but you'll know when you have them. They will feel right.

It doesn't really matter why you choose a card as your most appealing or least comfortable. Your choice might be because of the image, because of the colors, because of your personal associations with something in the card. *Whatever your reason*, these two cards are, at this particular moment, your two Power Cards. Let's consider them. (*Please* don't look them up in the second part of the book yet!)

As we go along with the various exercises like this one and the ones to follow, from time to time I shall suggest that you ask for information. Whenever I say "ask" in that way I mean to ask whatever or whoever you look to for guidance. It might be God or Goddess, the Christ Consciousness, your higher self, a spirit guide, your faery guide, or a faery on the card. It's up to you.

At this point I'd like to suggest that you keep an oracle journal, notes on what you are learning about the cards and Faery and the individual faeries and yourself. An excellent place to begin your notebook is with the following:

Look first at the card that appeals to you the most. Look at it carefully, and write down what you see there in response to the following questions.

1. What is the emotional atmosphere of the card? Does it seem peaceful? Happy? Sad? Loving? Lonely? Friendly? What else? If you don't know the answer, make a guess and write it down. Some cards have complex symbols, and it can be confusing at first to try to pick out one or a few simple attributes from the wealth available. If you have any difficulty with this, just close your eyes, hold the card, and ask for the first feeling word that comes to your mind. Don't worry about whether or not you know why your mind chose this word, just go with it for now. As you continue to look at the card, you might see more of the different archetypal energies and attributes shown in it. You might also see a deeper emotional tone than you did at first. Write those perceptions down as well.

2. What might the physical manifestation of this card's symbols be in someone's life? What aspect of life does this card symbolize to you? Could it be talking about better relationships? A special relationship? Solitude? More money? More fulfillment? More time for special activities? More things and possessions? Fewer? A simpler life? Chaos? Order? Activity? (What kind?) Health—good or bad or changing? What else? Again, if you don't think you know, close your eyes and ask for a word, while holding the card. Write down whatever word you get, or whatever image that comes into your mind.

3. What do you see in the card's symbols that might represent the card's mental characteristics? Is it complex or simple? Multi- or one-dimensional? Clear or confusing?

4. What are the spiritual characteristics of the card's symbols? Empathy, compassion, healing, awareness, teaching, questioning, or something else?

5. What do you find most appealing about this card?

6. Is there anything you find uncomfortable or unappealing about this card?

7. Have you any other ideas about or impressions of this card?

If you were unable to answer any of the questions above, I'd suggest that you take a break. Pet the cat or throw a stick for the dog, or go for a little walk or do something else that you enjoy for a few minutes. Loosen up. Sometimes we try so hard we block ourselves with the intensity of our energy. When that happens, we just need to let go a bit. Then come back and try it again in a more relaxed state of mind and body.

Once you've finished with the first card, let's look at the card that you felt most uncomfortable with. Go through the same questions above, but with a change in 5 and 6. The new versions of those two are:

5. What do you find most uncomfortable about this card?

6. Is there anything you find appealing or attractive about this card?

Please write down all of the answers to the questions before you continue reading.

The card that appeals to you the most tells you what you are trying to create in your life. This may be something you are consciously aware of working on, or it may have been hidden in your unconscious mind until this moment. Be as honest with yourself as you can. Look again for what the card shows—which may or may not be what you would prefer for it to show or what you thought you wanted.

People often argue about this card. It might show a peaceful scene of someone contemplative and solitary, suggesting that we have a desire for time for ourselves. Yet we may insist that we are trying to become involved in a relationship or expand our social life. If we allow them to, the cards tell us the truth about ourselves. They are, after all, just a magic mirror. They tell us about the things we have not let ourselves think—perhaps have not dared to consider or wish for. Begin to broaden your horizons, please, and consider all the possibilities. And remember that this is the card that you chose as the most appealing, so it surely represents something you deeply want, perhaps even need very much.

The card that makes you feel most uncomfortable tells you something about what you are having the most trouble dealing with in your life. It deals with your strongest inner conflict. It probably tells you quite a bit about what is hindering you from achieving the desires that are expressed in the card that appeals to you the most. It may also tell you about some of your blind spots. The being (or beings) on this card represents your most important teacher at this stage of your life.

Next, turn all the cards facedown. Let your hands and eyes wander over the backs of the cards. As you do this, focus part of your awareness on your breathing. Take deep, slow breaths down into your abdomen. As you do this, you will begin to notice that the cards are not all the same. It is true that they are made of the same paper and ink and show the same design on their backs, but they have subtle differences that are not necessarily visible to the eye. After a while one card will begin to draw you. It may pull very, very gently at your hand or your eyes—or even quite strongly. Pick up that card.

Answer the questions listed for the first card, the one you liked best, for this card as well.

Please do that before going on.

This card is a message from the universe (via your own higher self). It tells you something about how you can begin healing pain or resolving the issues shown by the uncomfortable card, and move closer to fulfilling the heart's desire expressed in the first, appealing card. Use the questions given earlier to look for the meaning in this card, and see what it tells you.

Have you noticed that you are reading the cards?

And have you noticed that you are doing it without looking anything up in the second part of this book, which contains the "definitions" of the cards? Maybe the magic truly is in you. Perhaps it's in Brian and his magical sight. Or it could be in me, and I've asked the magical questions that help you to find the answers you need to hear. Perhaps—and this seems most likely to me—it is in all three of us. It is certainly in Faery, and quite likely elsewhere as well. It might even be in the cards, too—it might be everywhere, just waiting to be used. We'll discuss that more later, but for now you might think about how you feel about being a magical being.

You can see from this that what matters for you is neither my interpretation of the cards nor Brian's nor anyone else's except yours. While I hope ours will enrich your interpretations, I certainly would not want ours to supersede yours. The only "right" interpretation for you is your own—and that will probably change at least a little each time you look at a card. Your personal response, the wealth of experience and awareness and humor and knowledge and wisdom and confusion that you bring to the cards is what matters.

To help you remember your own interpretations of the cards, I'd suggest you make yourself a reminder of the key words you discover for each card. Find a small notebook, one with a page for each card, and number the pages 0 through 65, along with the name of each card. Then keep the reminder notebook with your cards, and when you discover a new key word, add it to your notebook.

The more you learn and grow and the more you use the cards, the more you will see in them. The cards are magic mirrors in which we see aspects of ourselves. These aspects may be so weak as to be almost imperceptible or so strong as to be dominant characteristics in our personalities—or anywhere in between. We are all composed of the entire range of human experience.

Truly skilled readers can see everything they need to know in a scattering of dead leaves on the ground or in the twist of the stem of a flower. However, those of us who are less practiced than that will find that using these cards in cooperation with the faeries is very helpful in developing such skills. Having the faeries help, as a member of our Faery Oracle group says, is like having a "cheat sheet" that changes and offers new messages every time you look at it. Soon, with practice and their help, you'll be reading cards or leaves or clouds or chocolate chip cookies, whatever your métier is, like a pro.

So why use the cards at all? Because they are beautiful and enlighten our spirits. Because they are fun and lighten our hearts. Because they help illuminate and focus our attention and awareness. They help us to stay awake and aware in this world and Faery. And because faeries think they are great fun, too, and find this an easy, joyful way of reaching out to us.

Some of you will already have good communication with the faeries, but many others will wish to open and enhance that communication. Let's begin with how you can become better acquainted with Faery.

"The wings of flying faeries are symbolic of air, and their human or animal legs of earth. A shimmering, luminous quality is their fire aspect; the fluid aspect of shape-shifting represents water. Thus they make balanced connections among the four earthly elements and the four directions of the mystical winds. To all these, however, they add the magic of moonlight, the fifth faery element."
—Brian

Touching Faery

If you can't communicate directly with the faeries—or think you can't—this may be more helpful to you than anything else I can tell you about using this Oracle. I'm going to suggest several things in this chapter that may not seem to have anything directly to do with reading the cards, but in fact they are very helpful for developing your communication with the faeries. Developing that communication and learning to interact and share with the faeries is essential to reading the cards well.

For as long as I can remember, I have talked to, played with, worked with, and learned from the faeries. Imagine my surprise then when I began to write this book and realized how very few people know this about me: some of my friends, a few (but very few) of my family, and some, but by no means all, of my students. I was forced to realize that I was a "closet faery friend." This was a part of my life, a very important part, that was hidden from the general view.

Now, this might be understandable if I worked in a profession where keeping this a secret mattered, but I'm a healer and healers are expected to be weird. So, why . . . ?

Faeries keep their own secrets—and so do their friends. There have been good reasons why they have been so quiet for the past few centuries. Our world and the world of Faery have drawn apart in the natural tidal swings of the universe. While they were farthest apart, only a very few people had the sensitivity needed to sense across the gap. So Faery fell into disrepute with orthodox thinkers, resulting in disbelief in and denial of the otherworld realms for most of us.

A climate of doubt is difficult enough to deal with, but if we try to push people who are not ready into acknowledging Faery, we evoke hostility. Faeries are, of course, very energy sensitive. An atmosphere of hostility is extremely unpleasant for them, and they avoid it whenever possible. For this reason, true friends of Faery do not try to force belief or even awareness on those humans who are unready and unwilling.

Yet, now there are reasons why more and more people (human people, that is) are feeling moved to reconnect with the otherworld. The two worlds, ours and Faery, are drawing closer together again. The contact is easier, the doors open more easily. But, if we wish harmony between the worlds, it is important to meet Faery on its own terms and avoid projecting our own ideas and false beliefs onto it.

Many things about faery society are different from ours. Culture and manners differ. The things that are important and are considered to be common courtesy by humans and faeries are similar in some ways but vary widely in others. If we want a friendly response, we need to learn some things about faeries and what is important to them, just as we would of the inhabitants of a foreign human country we were visiting.

Where do we start if we want to become personal friends with the denizens of Faery? Or to enhance and expand the relationship we already have? I'm going to give you some suggestions to help you along your way, but you must understand that these are only suggestions. It is as if I am pointing to an invisible path that leads to a hidden gate. You are the one who has to actually find your way through. No human person can take you by the hand into Faery—and people who think they can are just kidding themselves and you. The suggestions I'm about to make worked for me and for many others, and I hope they will work for you. Even if they don't, you may well happen upon what does work for you while you're trying them. You have to discover your own way, but in doing so you will quickly find that you have the enthusiastic aid of the faeries themselves.

Well, fairies like to talk, so they like people who can be quiet and listen when that is appropriate. They speak in subtle voices, in hidden ways. If we aren't good at listening—and listening with more than just our ears—we won't be able to hear them. We need to listen with our hearts as well, and open ourselves to the subtle senses of emotion and empathy. They like us to be open enough so we can see or sense what is really there, more than just the obvious world of the physical eyes.

They like to play jokes, so we need a good sense of humor—good enough to laugh even when the joke is on us, as it frequently will be. I hope you won't mind their metaphorical custard pies, or taking the occasional mental pratfall while they giggle. If we can laugh at ourselves when we are laughed at by the faeries, the experience becomes a delightful one for all of us. Laughter creates a loving energy bond between those who laugh together, and it lightens our hearts.

To interact with Faery, it helps to realize that the otherworld is everywhere. It overlays our mundane world, enhancing it with magic and faery glamour when we open our eyes to see. The Faery counterpart of your own living room might be a garden, a meadow, a forest, a swamp, a rocky barren, a faery court, a dancing circle, or anything else—and the energy of that influences you, whether you are conscious of it or not. So wherever you are, the faeries are there too—or can be in the blink of an eye. You don't have to go anywhere special; where you already are *is* special. Be aware of that.

Singing with the Faeries

Faeries love to sing. They consider singing one of the great arts, an alchemy of the spirit. They have their own ideas about what constitutes song, and the one thing you can say for certain is that faery songs are always individual and original.

Faeries don't use what they call "canned music"—radios, tapes, any kind of recording. These bring "foreign" energy into the song and try to force the faeries to sing in a preprogrammed way rather than spontaneously and appropriately to the moment. The appropriate song raises our energy, makes us feel lighter and brighter. It also balances and raises the energy of the place in which we are singing. And it brings us more in harmony with both the place and the time—the significant, powerful moment of Now.

You may find it helpful to take several cards from the Oracle deck, choosing several faeries with whom you would like to sing. Put the cards where you can glance at them, if you wish, while you sing. You can even spread out the whole deck if you like.

Now, you can begin by just focusing on your breath—breathing in, breathing out. Open your mouth and let the outgoing breath make a sound, any sound the breath likes to make at this time. You will sometimes find that this sound changes from moment to moment. Just allow it to do so. With each breath, let the sound move and change as it wants to. Don't try to control or anticipate the sound—just let it happen.

When you first start to practice this, it may sound pretty weird, possibly even silly. That's all right, just let it. Remember to let your heart be light and playful. If you feel like giggling, do. Giggles are the grace notes of faery music. This fear of looking foolish to ourselves is one of the greatest obstacles to opening communication with the faeries for most of us. Another major obstacle is the fear of looking silly to others. That's why you are doing this by yourself. The greatest obstacle of all is believing we won't be able to do it and not trying.

After you have let the sounds just create themselves for a while, you will find that they begin to do interesting things. They may develop a beat or a melody. At first, beat and melody may be similar to music you are used to. However, the more you leave it free and the more you sing, the more unusual the song is likely to become. I'd suggest you don't try to do anything with this except to enjoy it. Faery songs balance and encourage joyful growth in the faeries themselves, the environment, and us. The more we do of this, the better we will feel.

Dancing

Another thing that fairies like is to dance, and they like people who dance with them. This doesn't mean that we have to be great dancers. We can dance with the faeries in a wheelchair, even if we are able do no more than nod our heads—in fact, even if we can do no more than beat our hearts. They are interested in and involved with the spirit, the energy of what we do, not primarily with the physical body. If we can dance with them with our energy, in our hearts, they will be delighted. There is an important point here: They ask only what we can give, but they do ask that much—given wholeheartedly.

As in singing with faeries, there are certain things that are better not to do. There are not very many of these things, and by now you may have discovered that singing is more fun without them. So is dancing. We don't do prepared or practiced dance steps, and we dance without other humans, especially at first, because whether we are pleased by our dancing or embarrassed by it, thinking about it is a terrible distraction from the real dance. Likewise, we don't use ready-made music. We follow our intuitive knowing and inner rhythm. We let our breath, bones, and muscles guide us. Our hearts can sense the dance even when our minds don't know it.

This kind of dancing comes straight from the creative heart of being. It does not have formal steps—it moves us like a small child dances. In fact, any two-year-old can and probably does do it. It is an out-flowing in motion of the energy of life. Flowers do it and so do trees—very slowly. Generally, we do it best if we start very slowly too.

So, how do we start? We might start by taking the faery portraits from the deck, putting them in a large circle around us, and inviting, aloud, the faeries to join us. Start with your breath, just your natural breath, nothing special or forced. Feel it move in your body, feel it move in the chest, and feel the more subtle movement deep in your abdomen. This is part of the energy dance of your body. While standing quietly, focus on being aware of your breath until you can feel how it alone moves your entire body, right down to your toes. Then let the body begin to move itself in response to the breath.

Breath is sacred; it transcends and permeates all of the worlds. Just rest into your body, your breath, your heartbeat, and your feelings. Let yourself *be* the movement. This takes practice and the practice takes patience—patience with ourselves. We can begin with just a gentle rocking or swaying; we might even start just with breathing. Try this: Let yourself focus on the movement of your pelvis, the sacral center, as you just breathe without other intentional movement, and allow movement to begin from there. You'll find that your body wants to rock or sway gently. Just let it.

See if you can keep your awareness in the center of your pelvis without caring too much about what the rest of your body is doing. Just let the pelvis do what it wants, however much or however little that is, and let the rest of the body follow it.

Some people may find it easier to start from the heart than from the pelvis. If so, do. But you will also need to learn to dance from the sacral center, in the center of the pelvis, because that is our connection with magic and power, while the heart is our connection with love and joy. In time, you will get good enough at it to dance wholly from both centers, equally and simultaneously.

A helpful thing to remember is that, if we are losing our balance and stumbling or falling, we are not fully tuned into faery dancing. Let go more of the conscious control—thinking, planning, anticipating. Slow down. Dancing with faeries is a kind of freedom from the mind and a renewal of the spirit. We feel better at the end of it. We do not have strained muscles or bruises, either of the body or of the spirit.

All right, now you know that the first steps on the path to Faery can be dancing ones. When the faeries see you making an attempt to be with them, they'll reach out to you as well. If you find that your heart is feeling lighter or that you feel like giggling or that your blood seems to be bubbling and fizzing in your body instead of just flowing along in its usual way, you know for certain that you have been dancing with the faeries. Perhaps your fingers or your nose will tingle; perhaps there will be some other sign. Enjoy the fizzy feeling!

"Faeries are not a fantasy but a connection to reality."
—*Brian*

Reading the Cards

In this chapter, we shall be considering how you can read the cards for your own interest and enlightenment. Later on, in "Reading the Oracle for Others" and "Faery-Style Readings," we'll look at how you can share the Faeries' Oracle with others, but for now let's see how you can use the Oracle to gain insight into your own life and help you to make better decisions.

There are some simple things you can do to make yourself a better reader of any oracle, regardless of whom you are reading it for. In addition to greatly improving our abilities as readers, these things help us more easily communicate with Faery and lead lives that are more balanced and enjoyable. They are also all things that faeries enjoy doing with us. These things are meditation, earthing, centering, and connecting.

To *meditate* is to practice simple mental exercises in concentration.

Earthing (or *grounding*) is connecting with the earth, exchanging your energy with hers, and allowing your energy to be cleansed and restored by her.

To be *centered* is to be balanced in your own being, looking out at the world from your inner position of power.

Connecting is establishing rapport with the higher self, Faery, and the powers that be—whoever you relate to in the higher realms.

If you don't know how to do any of these very important things, the information begins on page 181.

Here are the steps to follow when reading for yourself.

1. Make certain you are earthed, centered, connected, and in a relaxed meditative state.

2. Request aid and guidance from Faery in doing the reading.

Just do it, that's all. That's easy, isn't it? "Please" is a nice word, too.

3. Define the question to be addressed in the reading.

Focusing the Reading: With any reading, it is very helpful to start with a clear, appropriate question; indeed, the trickiest part of doing a reading with any type of oracle is in asking the right kind of question. Each card has great quantities of information to offer, applying to many different aspects of life. The energies of each card might apply to the querent's health, work, relationships, recreation, psychological or spiritual growth, or anything. (The querent is the person asking the question. It may be you yourself or it may be someone else.)

The questions are what bring focus and clarity to the reading. The fuzzier and more general the question, the more mysteriously "oracular" and confusing the answers tend to be. Of course, as we become more experienced, this is less of a problem, partly because we learn to ask questions more clearly.

A simple question like, "What do I need to do to improve my health?" or "How can I improve my relationship with my [boss/partner/children/whomever]?" immediately tells us what the message of the faery on the card is about. Let's look at the basics of asking good, answerable questions.

Be Specific: Be as precise as you can in your question. Name the relevant people and places whenever possible. Identify the situation or issue clearly. Be specific about the time frame—"within the last six months" or "in the next two months" or "next Tuesday," for example.

Put First Things First: Make certain you are asking first questions first. For example, asking, "How should I deal with the boss on my new job?" when you don't yet have a new job—and therefore don't actually have a new boss—is not useful and may be misleading. The future is not fixed and readings only give information about probabilities, not about a fixed fate. So the first question here really needs to be about preparing for and then finding a new job. Once the job has been found, *then* we can talk about dealing with the boss.

Often when we find that a reading is just not making sense or we are getting inconsistent answers, it is because we are asking the wrong questions first. We tend to get our minds fixed upon certain things—goals, decisions, outcomes—and when we do that, we often start our questioning in the middle, assuming that we know what goes before. At least half of being a good oracle reader is knowing what questions to ask. Really good questions often answer themselves and the faeries just confirm the answer.

Choose Active and Not Passive Questions: Here are some examples of passive questions:

Will I be rich?

Will I be loved?

How will this situation turn out?

Passive questions assume that we have neither choice nor responsibility in creating our futures. They expect the universe to do things *to* us, rather than understanding that our lives are a process that we co-create with the universe. These questions tend to be based on an assumption that there is nothing we can do to make our lives better or happier. The true usefulness of an oracle is not to predict our nonexistent fate. So-called fate is actually a combination of the events beyond our control and of what we choose to make of them—even if we simply sit there and do nothing. That, too, is a choice.

An oracle helps us to discover more about ourselves, our lives, and our relationships so that we can make better, more conscious choices rather than just letting things happen to us. The more we frame our question so that we get the information that will help us to do that, the more useful the reading is. For example, instead of asking, "Will I get the job?" we might want to ask a series of questions.

We could begin with "Would this job with [X Company] be good for me at this time?" Assuming the answer is yes, we might then ask, "What can I do to make my chances of getting this job with [X Company] better?" Do you see the difference? Passive questions assume that things are already decided and that we can't do anything about them. (If you believe that, the faeries certainly have surprises in store for you!) Active questions assume that you can take part in co-creating your future with the universe, and that you have choices about your present path and your future.

Try for Clarity: Above all, do not expect to get a clear answer to a muddled question. If you can't ask a clear, simple question, it is because you really don't know what the problem is. Think again until you have your question clear. There is, of course, no certainty that simple questions will have simple answers, but it is at least a possibility.

This may seem obvious when you think about it, but it is important to ask and clarify your question before you choose the layout and deal the cards. Then hindsight does not become confused with foresight, generating a terrible muddle.

4. Shuffle the cards, if desired, while focusing on the question.

5. Choose the cards, placing them facedown on the work surface.

Once again, find what works best for you. Some people like to shuffle the cards, cut them into three stacks, stack them again in a different order, and deal the cards from the top of the deck. Other people have other systems. I like to make a smooth arc of cards (see page 43). Then I choose the cards from anywhere in the arc, putting them *facedown* into the chosen card layout (see "Basic Card Spreads," starting on page 36). Let's say, for example, that you are doing a simple three-card reading of past, present, and potential on a question. You would choose three cards individually from anywhere in the arc and now have a row of three cards facedown in front of you.

6. One by one, turn the cards over, acknowledging the presence of the faery shown on the card and asking them what they wish to tell you.

Begin with Card One. *Decide in advance* whether you are going to flip the cards end for end or turn them over sideways. The cards have different meanings if they are upside down than they do when they are oriented the right way up, so it makes a difference how they are turned over. People often want to turn them "the right way around" to get a "better" reading, but this distorts the reading. Choose the way you want to turn them, and then stick to it. That will eliminate a lot of confusion, especially when you are reading for yourself.

7. From the cards read the faery messages and think about how the messages relate to the position of the card in the layout, if you are using more than one card.

As you turn the card over you say something like, "This first card tells me about something in the past that I need to consider regarding this question." Then you look at the card, ask the faery for guidance, and *listen*.

This is a special kind of listening—you do it with your whole body and with your whole self, using all of your senses. Notice what your eyes are drawn to in the card. This might be one of the main figures or one of the others. It might even be a detail such as something held by one of the faeries or something in the background. Ask yourself what this eye-catcher is and what it symbolizes or represents or suggests in regard to the question. (See the "Recommended Sources" section in the back of this book for a good book on interpreting symbols and images.)

Notice the feelings in your own body and whether or not they have changed in some way over the last few minutes. Notice any sounds or scents that you haven't been aware of before. All of these things *may* be

*"All faeries appear on the threshold
of what is and what is to be."*
—*Brian*

faery communications. It may not—probably *won't*, especially in the beginning—be something so simple as a clear faery voice. Faery messages come in subtle ways. The faeries might direct your eyes to something that is a symbol of what they want to communicate. Or you may get a whiff of a scent borne on an otherworld breeze. What does that scent remind you of? What feelings does it evoke in you? Or your eyes might keep coming back to a particular detail on the cards. What does that image say or symbolize to you? Images, strange or mundane, may pop up in your mind, songs might start to sing themselves in your ears. Listen to them carefully. Note them, ask yourself what they mean, what they tell *you* through the rich symbolism in your own mind. It's like interpreting the elements of a dream. Each image, each detail, has its own meaning—some obvious, some obscure, but all significant. As you do this, it often helps to clarify your thoughts if you describe them aloud.

Feel free to say whatever is coming up for you, regardless of whether it makes sense to you or not. Sometimes the faeries are just silly while they are establishing the connection. Let the images and sensations run *through* you. Recognize them and wait for more. Clarity will come—and it comes more often and more quickly with practice. As you get better at working with the free-flowing energy/information of the faeries, you will find that more and more often it forms some wonderful connection between the faery message and what is going on in your life.

In addition, of course, you need to think about who the faery is, what the faery's special field of interest is, and how that might apply to the issue at hand.

When you get stuck in this reading process, which happens even to experienced readers, just pause and close your eyes. Breathe. Earth. Center. Connect. Remember what it felt like when you were dancing and singing with the faeries back in the "Touching Faery" chapter. When you feel centered, connected, and back in the meditative state, open your eyes and look at the card again. Don't rush; quietly take your time. Use the silence to listen, and go on from there.

As you read the second card, begin to look at how what it says might relate to the information in the first card. We are considering the second card as the present, so how is the present described by the faeries affected by the card of the past? Then, go on to the third card, seeing it as both a potential outcome and a guide to how that outcome might occur.

(When we get to "Basic Card Spreads," we'll consider what you might want to do if the potential outcome is undesirable.)

While you are doing the things described above, notice any physical signals—itches, twitches, tickles, or other sensations—or perhaps just a sense of energy somewhere in your body. These signals are ephemeral; they happen for a while and then change, but they do tell us that something magical is going on deeper in consciousness. They give us verification of connection with the faeries and are a kind of feedback from our own bodies and energy fields. The messages that come *with* these signals tend to be especially important. You will find with experience that psychic information has a characteristic feeling for you, and once you have learned to recognize those feelings and sensations, you will feel more confident about your reading. Eventually we outgrow the need for these signals, but they are useful in the beginning.

8. Summarize the story or theme of the reading for yourself.

A reading tells a story, and it is very useful to briefly summarize that story for yourself at the end of the reading. To be most helpful, this summary needs to be as simple as possible. For our imaginary three-card reading, you might say something like, "So in summary, I see that in the past I benefited from [or were hurt by/traumatized by/confused about/bogged down in] X [or by experiencing X]. That is affecting me in the present as I try to deal with Y by repeating this old pattern [or by reacting against this previous experience or whatever]. Now, in order to move forward, I will find it very helpful to do Z [or take a Z attitude or whatever], which will help me to achieve my goals in a focused way."

The summary is important because it helps you remember the reading later. The bare framework provides something to which your memory can link the details. It also makes certain that you have the core message clear in your own mind and haven't become lost in details.

9. Thank those who have helped you.

As we shuffle the cards and put them back into a neat pile, we can thank the faeries for sharing and bless them. Faeries, like anyone else, appreciate being thanked for their help, but we also need to realize that thanking them is important *to us*. It grounds the energy and information of the reading in this world so we can benefit from it. Through gratitude we accept this energy into our own beings and lives. Also, this will help you have a feeling of completion about the reading.

10. Close down the reading.

Develop your own ritual for ending the reading. This needs to include earthing, centering, and connecting. It also needs to include letting go of the reading. Again, each of us has to find what works best for ourselves, but those elements need to be a part of it. What I do is to make certain I am finished with the reading, and then gather up the cards. I shuffle them one last time as I repeat my thanks to whoever helped me for the guidance I've received. Then, I put the cards away and jot down some notes about the reading in my Oracle journal. And lastly, I simply go and do something else for a while. This is a good time for a break for tea or petting the cat or doing something like going for a walk or some other physical activity.

What is happening here is that we are switching from the meditative, intuitive state of consciousness, in which we do readings, back to our normal state. If we do not do this clearly and cleanly, we wind up becoming vague, confused, and never quite being where we really need to be mentally. This is one of the most common problems readers have, especially beginners. It is also a major difficulty for people who have been improperly trained or who have chosen to ignore the need for closure for *each* reading, even if several are being done in succession. When we get the beginnings and endings of reading right, the rest tends to work well.

Whew!

There now! That wasn't so complicated, was it? At first, it may seem a little so, but with practice most of the steps become automatic, like drifting down a river in a canoe without having to paddle any more than just enough to keep on course. This is a very natural, organic style of reading, and it is pleasing to the faeries. The more you practice it, the more you will find that it is very enjoyable. There is the occasional reading where something is being dealt with that is difficult to face, and though these readings can't really be described as *fun*, they can still leave you with a sense of satisfaction at having done as well as you can, given the circumstances.

Reading for yourself is the hardest kind of reading. If you can do that, you can read for anyone. This is because the closer we are to the subject of a reading, the more difficult it is to be confident of our objectivity and openness to truth. Do not be discouraged if you find it hard. Try practicing with other people, perhaps exchanging readings, for a while (see

"Reading the Oracle for Others," page 188). Reading for others is *much* easier than reading for yourself, especially in the beginning, but as you become more skilled you will find reading for yourself becomes easier as well. However, I would recommend that when you want an accurate reading for yourself on a subject that you feel very strongly about or that is very important, you consider getting an objective interpretation from an experienced reader. Most professional readers read for themselves, but even they double-check their readings on important matters with someone else.

> *"Faeries show us flow and the possibilities of change.*
> *They show us clarity and insight and the fact that everything*
> *is connected and that we are all part of one another."*
> —Brian

Ethics

Last but not least, there are some very important ethical and karmic issues that arise when we work with oracles. Most important, we must not invade the privacy of others. Oracles should not be used to peep into the bedroom windows or private lives of others. Just because we may want to know something doesn't mean that it is necessarily ethical for us to seek that information psychically any more than it is to read other people's mail, listen to their phone calls, or snoop around in any other way.

In general, questions that ask about the personal feelings or the private behavior of others are the ones most likely to fall into inappropriate areas. Consider carefully the ethical implications of the questions that are being asked. Would you consider it appropriate to answer them if you were speaking from the standpoint of an ordinary friend with personal knowledge of the people involved? If we violate ethical principles or privacy in our readings, the universe and the faeries will be very helpful about teaching us more appropriate behavior. Many people think that karma is the universe punishing us. It isn't, though it may sometimes feel like that. It is simply the universe (and perhaps some of those mentioned in "The Faery

Challengers") helping us to learn the consequences of inappropriate and unethical behavior.

These are the main steps you need to know about reading the Faeries' Oracle for yourself. Practicing them will deepen your insight into your own life and enhance your connections with the otherworld of Faery and all of its delights. Next we'll be learning some more detailed information about card layouts and how we can explore our lives, choices, and options with the cards.

Basic Card Spreads

The ways in which we lay out the cards for readings (called a *layout* or a *spread*) can be divided into two basic types: layouts you learn from a teacher or a book and ones you create yourself. There are dozens, hundreds, thousands of spreads you can learn from others. Just remember that all of these were created by someone—just like you—and none of them are The Only Right Way to read. You can find many books that offer a great variety of structured layouts, and they can be very helpful. (See "Recommended Sources" in the back for suggestions.)

Apart from describing the basic one- and three-card readings to help you get started here, I'm not going to cover territory that has been gone over so very well elsewhere. In the next chapter, we'll focus on how to do original, creative, custom-made faery-style readings, but first, let's look at the basics of getting started with one- and three-card readings.

One-Card Readings

One-card readings are good for asking general, open-ended questions like, "What primary thing do I need to learn from this [specific] experience?" They are also good for general daily readings, where you are simply asking for what you need to be aware of that day. They can also be helpful when you want a very simple, specific response to a question like, "What is the very first thing I need to work on to improve my health?"

One-card readings are *not* good for simple yes/no questions or questions where you need to consider things like the past, present, and potential of a person, issue, event, or situation. They are also obviously not as

good as multiple-card readings for questions about making choices or dealing with alternative possibilities.

I find that one-card readings usually work best for simple personal
growth and learning or for exceedingly simple questions. Formulating a
clear and concise question is the key to using one-card readings success-
fully. They are especially useful when we need to simplify an issue, cutting
to the bone. For example, we could ask, "What asset do I have that will be
the most help in dealing with this situation?" The card drawn will then tell
us *specific* helpful things about which strengths and attitudes we need to
bring into play to improve the situation. (The faeries *do* like the expression
"bring into play.")

Many people, including myself, like to draw a card for the day, as
just mentioned. The faery of the card tells us what we would benefit from
looking for and thinking about. For example, the Faery Who Was Kissed by

*"Angels are said to be the thought forms
of God, and heavenly messengers.
They are the form builders of the
universe and the embodiments of
divine will, perched at the top of the
continuum of spiritual beings flowing
downward to the smallest of faery
creatures. All angels mediate cosmic
and spiritual forces and will come
to our aid when we call upon them.
Angels could be called grown-up
faeries—or, to put another way,
faeries are little angels."*
—Brian

the Pixies (Card 21) might suggest watching for and considering love expressed in both subtle and obvious ways, both given and received. Gloominous Doom (Card 56) might recommend that we be aware of self-pity in ourselves or others and the effects of that attitude on whatever is happening.

These faery exercises are all good training in understanding the potentials of the individual faeries of the Oracle cards. They also help us to develop insight into ourselves and others, and they encourage us to respond to events and people in new ways because we have seen them in a new light.

Another useful question is "What is the message from the faeries I might beneficially consider putting into action today?" The faery of the card we draw may suggest that we consider taking action on something in particular. Ilbe (Card 41) might suggest that we do something to help a dream come true—our own or someone else's. The Singer of Courage (Card 8) might recommend that we go ahead and take a risk we have feared—and help us feel the courage to do it.

One member of the Oracle e-mail group, who helped with this book, suggested an altogether different approach to a one-card reading—a meditative rather than analytical one. She calls it the "cooked spaghetti spread" and says it is "analogous to throwing cooked spaghetti up in the air. If it sticks to the ceiling, it's done! Spend twenty minutes or so meditating on that card and see what arises. No muss, no fuss, no rules. I find it helpful for situations when you know something needs more conscious, concrete attention but you haven't a clue what sort, or in what way. If I let the card lead the way, I often am given something very new to look at, beyond the range of the experience of the question."

She also suggests approaching a card by asking, "What do I have to say to this card?" This can allow a free-flowing dialogue that may well come up with insights, images, and ideas that may form an entirely new approach or understanding, both of ourselves and of the issue.

As you can see, dear reader, there are a lot of things you can do with just one card. I'm certain that you can find many more, just as the people of the Oracle e-mail group have. (See "Recommended Sources" in the back of the book for information about joining us on-line.) One reason I have put their comments and suggestions in this book is that I want you to clearly understand that I don't have the final or even the only word here—the faeries do, and *they* speak to whoever is willing to listen. *Your* input and contributions and card-spread inventions are also important, even if you are "just a beginner." Of course, the other reason those comments are here is because they are really useful suggestions and observations about the faeries.

Three-Card Readings
There are many things you can do with simple all-of-your-ducks-in-a-row, three-card layouts.

Probably the most common three-card layout is the simple (1) past, (2) present, and (3) future. This is a useful way of looking at many issues, situations, and questions. The "past" can tell us about the unresolved issues and attitudes that are influencing the way we handle the matter at hand. The "present" can give us information about a wide variety of things—hidden aspects of the situation, unconscious attitudes that affect our choices, the external forces or conditions that bear on the issue, or others. The "future" tells us about the *probable* outcome of the issue if people and things continue moving in the same direction they have been, but it is important to remember that they don't *have* to move that way—and they may not. The future reading is more focused on potential possibilities than on fate, because it is doubtful that fate has much to do with our futures at all. However, looking at possibilities and potentials is extremely useful, as long as we remember that this is all they are.

Another useful three-card reading is the basic yes/no spread. When the cards are turned over, three upright cards mean "very likely yes" while three reversed cards mean "very likely no"—simple, isn't it? Of course, two up and one down tell us "probably yes" while the reverse tells us "probably no." In all cases, the reversed cards also tell us "why not" and the upright cards tell us "why yes." If the answer is something we want to change, we can draw companion cards, asking, "Is there anything I can do to change this?" A reverse card indicates that the answer is "probably not" and tells us more about the situation and the reason why not. An upright companion card not only indicates that there is a potential for change but also suggests something of how that change might be brought about. There is more on the use of companion cards later.

I must have done hundreds, possibly thousands of three-card readings, with many variations on the theme. But here are some examples from the Oracle group.

One member says she often uses this layout: "Card One represents here and now—the mess I've gotten into, or just the plain, old, "I'm stuck here." Card Three represents where I want to be. Card Two represents the bridge I need to cross to get out of One and into Three.

In another of this teacher's favorite three-card readings, "Card One (which is chosen faceup) represents what I want or where I want to be or what I want to accomplish. The other cards are chosen facedown. Card Two represents my greatest challenge to achieving Card One. Card Three represents the first step I can take to get past the challenge—and by "first step" I mean a real, concrete thing, not something nebulous. Card Three helps one to begin a plan of action."

Another on-line Oracle reader says, "I liked the past, present, and future theme that I have seen other people use, but I decided that another very important threesome is the body, the mind, and the spirit." We can use this to look at a particular issue and how it is affecting us physically, mentally, and spiritually. This can also help us to identify inner conflicts and give us guidance about how we might resolve them.

A third member of the group suggested, "Card One can be chosen faceup, and it describes the situation or is descriptive of the querent. Cards Two and Three, chosen from the deck as shuffled, could represent possible outcomes of the two options that are almost always available to us—the option of continuing to work within the situation and the option of moving on."

Finally, yet another provided two good card spreads. First, "My daily three-card spread is used to suggest my daily focus for work, play, and people, respectively." This is an interesting expansion of the daily one-card reading. What subjects would be appropriate for your own days?

He also uses a three-card spread to solve problems. "Whenever I need quick help with a specific problem, usually work related, or for a jog when I'm blocked or stuck in a creative or artistic activity, I lay out three cards. They each answer one of the three questions—Card One: What is important? Card Two: What am I missing? Card Three: What should I do?"

As you can see, we all just make them up to suit our needs of the moment. Please feel free to make them up yourself. The key is to look at the question and ask yourself what information you need to answer it. We'll consider more on creating layouts to suit our questions later on, but first . . .

Reversed Cards

When you turn a card over and it is upside down, that is called a *reversed card*, and it indicates a variation on the faery message it would otherwise suggest. Sometimes it means that the message is the opposite of that of the upright card. Other times it may suggest a block or a delay in the fulfillment of the energy or message of that particular card. Or it could indicate resistance to its message. I've given "starter readings" and "reversed" readings for all of the cards in Part Two, but those are not hard and fast definitions. Stay earthed, centered, connected, in a meditative state, and let the faeries help you to find the most appropriate definitions for each card, reversed or upright.

Predicting the Future

The future has not happened yet and it is not fixed. In real life, practically everything is subject to change without notice.

Whenever we ask something about the future, the answer we get is not the Absolute Truth. There isn't yet any absolute truth for us to get. What we do get (assuming that we are not so emotionally involved that our own unconscious desires or fears warp the answer) is information on the *most probable outcome* of the present situation—provided that everyone involved continues to behave in the way that they normally act.

If we don't like that answer, we can ask if the result can be changed by any action on the part of the person receiving the reading. If the answer is yes (as it often is), we will probably want to ask for alternative courses of action and their most likely results. If the answer is no, the person asking the question will probably benefit from some intuitive counseling to help her to deal with this probable outcome in the way that will be most beneficial for her. If we are reading for ourselves, this may be the point at which we want to seek help from another reader.

It is a good idea to always remind ourselves and make it clear to others at the beginning of a reading that the future is not fixed, that it is subject to change without notice, that future predictions are only projections based on what is happening now, and that such information should be used wisely and not regarded as infallible. We have free will and free *won't*, and to a great extent we get to choose our future.

What you really get when you ask about the future are *probabilities*—not fate or certainties. This is one of the reasons why very few psychics get rich betting on the horses. Rather than looking for fate, we will do much better if we use the Oracle to look for insight into ourselves and others and for ways that we can make the most of our lives, whatever happens.

Companion Cards

Sometimes we draw a card that raises another question rather than answering one. Or perhaps we draw a card and the meaning is quite unclear to us and no amount of earthing and centering and listening makes it any more clear. When this happens, we can simply choose a *companion card* to clarify the meaning of the baffling one. For example, when Ilbe (Card 41) shows up in a reading he may be speaking of lost hopes. If he is, we may recognize right away just which forlorn and near-forgotten hope Ilbe is talking about—or we may not. If we don't get it after we've thought about it a for bit, the simplest thing to do is to draw a companion card from the remaining deck.

This card clarifies the card in the original reading that you find unclear. For example, suppose you draw Oengus Journeyman (Card 15) as the companion card for Ilbe. Oengus might represent a journey that was longed for but thought impossible, or he might represent moving or traveling or stepping out into a new life in some other significant way. With that much of a clue, we probably will be able to identify the lost hope and relate it to the rest of the reading.

If you find yourself drawing more than one or two companion cards in a reading, something is not right. There are several possibilities. You may have become ungrounded, uncentered, and disconnected and are unable to pick up the subtle faery messages. If so, you need to earth, center, and refocus yourself, moving back into the meditative state in which we read. Alternatively, the original question may have been too complex or unclear and needs to be restructured. Or you may be resisting the message of the reading, probably unconsciously, which suggests that you might need to get another reader to help you work through this. Often we need the help of others to clarify our confusion and to see past our own blocks.

Too many companion cards start to fragment a reading, losing us in details and making it harder to understand the overall picture. When this happens, you might try refocusing the question, refocusing yourself, and reshuffling the cards. The very best readings have a simple directness to them. They may go into complex issues and contain profound thoughts, but in the end they should simplify and clarify, not confuse and complicate. It is often better to do several small card spreads, each in response to its own clear question and keeping each mini-reading-within-a-reading to one aspect of the main issue, than it is to get lost in one huge muddled layout that spreads over the table and onto the floor. (Don't laugh; I've seen it happen. Well, all right, go ahead and laugh if you like. It's as funny as a pie in the face.)

Bear in mind the faery version of the KISS principle: Keep It Simple, Sweetwings!

Arcing the Cards

Now that you've learned a few of the basic skills of reading, here is a fancy bit. It has nothing to do with your skills as a reader, but faeries like it and it often impresses anyone you might be reading for, which sometimes helps him to be more receptive to what you say. It may even help to give you a little more confidence, even though it is just a bit of showmanship with a merry, zappy energy to it—which faeries quite enjoy.

These are the directions for a right-handed person. If you're left-handed, just reverse this.

First, you need a carpet or a piece of velvet or some other smooth but nappy surface to work on. This won't work well on a slick surface like a varnished or glass tabletop or on a very rough surface like a deeply cut carpet. Shuffle or mix the cards. Put the deck, *facedown*, near the right side of the working area. Put your right hand on the cards so that your fingers are *almost* touching the surface on the side to your far right; then just gently swing your arm across so that your hand moves in an arc across the surface, letting the bottom cards slide out from under your fingers as you do. The cards fan open.

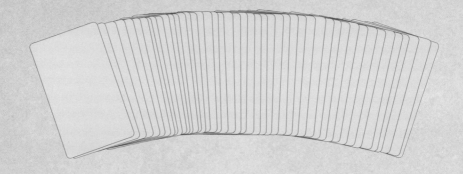

One hint about arcing the cards: When they stick or have big irregularities in the arc, it may be that the surface you are working on is too slick and it doesn't "grab" the cards properly. Otherwise, it might be that you are not calm, grounded, and centered while you are trying to make your swing. Just pause for a moment, gather the cards up again, and take a deep, slow breath or two. Then try again. Practice definitely makes us much better at this. It also helps us to check ourselves for being earthed and centered as we begin the reading.

I usually find that, when I get it right, there is a faery giggle that goes with it, a little energy surge of delight from the faeries. It lightens my spirit and illuminates the reading. It always makes me smile a little, and it's a good time to take the opportunity to mentally thank the faeries for being present and joining in.

One More . . .
Here is another three-card reading for you to try. This one is about relationships—not just love affairs but any kind of relationship. It could be two people working on a project, boss and employee, lovers, parent and child, neighbors, or whatever. Each of the cards, One, Two, and Three, represents one of the following aspects of the subject:

1. What the other needs from the relationship.
2. What the relationship needs from both.
3. What you need from the relationship.

Having looked at that, you could expand and deepen the reading by drawing three more cards, placing them below the first three. The second set of three tells us the following:

1. What the other brings to the relationship.
2. What the relationship offers to both.
3. What you bring to the relationship.

Oops! That was a six-card reading. I suppose we'd better go on to the next thing because we aren't really looking at more complex readings until Part Three. So far we have only considered reading the cards for ourselves, but later on we shall consider reading for others and using the special faery-style readings.

Before you move on to Part Three you may want to play with the cards themselves for a while. In Part Two we begin to look at the individual faeries of the Oracle and see how their energies and ways of being relate to the readings we have just discussed. I know you must be as eager to play with the faeries as they are to be with you. As you become more acquainted with them, you will see how they illuminate the meaning of our lives and bring insights to us in a way that balances the metaphysical and physical, the practical and the spiritual, as all good oracles must do.

Part Two

Reading the Faery Cards

Getting to know a faery is easy. Just listen with your whole self

Introducing Certain Faeries

In the beginning of my part of creating this oracle deck, I sat on the floor with copies of about 120 of Brian's paintings spread around me, and I invited all of the faeries depicted (and anyone else who wanted to join in) to help in making the decisions about who would be part of the Oracle. (Of course, *all* faeries are part of the Faeries' Oracle, even if they are not on the cards, but that's another book.) I also asked them to tell me how they wanted me to describe the working of their Oracle to you. They were excited and very enthused about this project, and discussed at length whose pictures should be in the deck, changing their minds at frequent intervals and then changing them back again.

At their direction, I arranged and rearranged the paintings in stacks and rows and circles. This went on all afternoon. And evening. And late into the night. It seemed to amuse them a great deal. My cats, who had been excited by the presence of all those faeries at once, began to murmur complaints. About two in the morning, I suggested (yet again) that we do this in some sort of logical manner. I asked if they could define groups that I might put them in to make the selection process easier.

They shook their heads and looked doubtful, saying, *"You people will get it all wrong. People have hierarchies, and we don't. Some of us are bigger and some smaller, but we each do our own tasks, and we are each as important as any other. Humans get that wrong when they think about us."*

I sighed and picked up the paintings, thanking the faeries for their help. Then the cats and I went to sleep.

A week or so later, I again asked who was going to be in the deck and got much the same runaround. We had a good time playing with the paintings while they admired themselves and each other, but we didn't get anywhere with the selection process. However, they had obviously been thinking things over because they nodded when I asked if they could help me to put the different faeries into groups or categories, just to help people learn who they are and remember them.

"Yes," a Topsie-Turvet said firmly. *"You may divide us into three groups— the Aliu and Alyshu."*

I waited expectantly for a moment, and then asked, "And the third?"

They all burst out laughing at me. I had to laugh, too; I'd been caught by another daft faery joke.

We left the whole subject for quite a while as I wrote bits of the first part of this book. Then Constance, our editor, asked me for a list of the cards. Eeep! I started looking through the paintings again. Almost miraculously, they seemed to divide themselves into two sets: the ones in the deck and the ones not. Then the ones in the deck grouped themselves into five sets of thirteen each. I counted again, and yes, there were thirteen each, sixty-five total. By this time, there were exhausted faeries sprawled everywhere in the room, and I felt elated but ready to collapse. *"Don't forget,"* someone muttered from behind a cushion, *"there is another card—a blank one for people's own faery guide."*

I worked out what five thirteens add up to (hard to do on fingers) and added in the special blank card, and there were sixty-six altogether—a nice round number. I thought about the numerological meaning of 66—the Master Caregiver, the generous spirit, who seeks beauty, harmony, and balance. It is also the number of responsibility and ethics. How appropriate this is to the Oracle, which is about the faeries helping us and us helping each other and the faeries to live more wisely and more happily and more beautifully. Then, when you do the numerological process of reducing the number to one digit (6+6=12, 1+2=3), you get Three—the number of creativity and joy and communication. Very apt for *this* oracle.

As I considered the number of the cards, I also wondered if the faeries would agree to putting numbers on the individual cards to make it easier for you to look them up. A pixie peered down from the top of a bookshelf and said, *"You can use numbers, if you like, as long as you remember to tell them that the numbers don't mean anything at all—except when they do."*

I hope you will bear that in mind. However, I feel compelled to mention that they have been very picky about who got which numbers, and certain faeries kept changing places within their sets until the last possible moment.

From this, you can perhaps begin to imagine the fun we had in writing the "definitions" of the cards. Some were quite certain what they wanted to say and others were not. I can sympathize with this because I feel the same way when a publisher or someone else asks me for a biographical sketch. What one says depends on who one is talking to, and it's very hard to say something brief that is suitable for everyone. So I wasn't too surprised when I asked Fairy Nuff what he'd like me to write about him, and he said, *"Nothing."*

"Come on," I said, patiently coaxing. "People need to know something about you."

"Then I shall tell them myself. I don't want you to pin me down with words like a poor dead butterfly on a collector's board. I don't want to be all word wrapped and trapped. I want them to ask me and then to listen to me. I want to be friends with them, and we can't be friends if they won't listen."

I had to admit the justice of his point of view. So, the group of faeries and I finally reached an agreement. I would report Fairy Nuff's words here so that you would know how he felt, and then the other faeries would help me write something about themselves to help you get started on understanding them. However, I must also ask you, please, to ask *them* for information and advice when you are using their oracle, because what is said here is just the veriest beginning of the things they would like to tell you. They have far more to say than we can say here—even if I were allowed to write a book so big that you'd need a wheelbarrow to carry it.

I might just sneakily mention here that Fairy Nuff's attitude tells you a lot about him. If you ask, I'm sure he will explain—and that's fair enough. He is on Card 46.

Lastly, the faeries want me to re-remind you that no denizen of Faery is better or more important than another. It doesn't matter who is oldest or who is biggest; each has its own responsibility and is as important as any other, from the most ancient sidhe to the tiny faeries who encourage the sunflower seeds to grow in my garden—and yours. Each is a part of the great tapestry, the fabric of the universe (which is probably denim, to judge from its hard-wearing qualities), and all threads are equally important, including ours—yours and mine. If anyone were suddenly to cease to exist, the whole thing might unravel—or so they tell me. You can believe what you like, but I rather believe them.

Now, let's go play with faeries!

"Each person's sojourn in Faery is highly individual and unique. Each traveler moves through a very different symbolic and emotional landscape. Thus the meaning of a painting reveals itself only individually, changing from viewer to viewer."

—Brian

The Zero Card

Card 0 – The Guide
Guidance. Direct Communication with Faery.

This card has been left blank for you to draw your own Faery Guide on. Some people may have a clear mental image of their personal guide to Faery, but if you don't have that yet there are a couple of things you can try. First, try doing some loose sketches in a meditative state, asking your personal guide to help you draw. That will probably work, but if it doesn't, ask to be given a symbol to represent that fairy, and then just go with the first thing that comes to mind, whatever it is.

By drawing your Faery Guide (or its symbol) on the card, you personalize and attune the deck, connecting the energy of the cards and the faeries on them with your own energy. Some people go through elaborate rituals with their tarot decks and oracles to get an energy connection between themselves and the deck, but that is unnecessary with this one. All you need to do here is to include your own Faery Guide in the deck, and everything is taken care of.

Starter Reading Both this and the reverse reading are something you will need to work out with your Faery Guide. Please note that this, like all the starter readings on the other faeries' cards, are subject to change without notice. That's how faeries are, and I think when you get used to working that way with them, you will find it a very rewarding experience—and fun.

Reversed This card reversed often means you aren't listening. It may mean other things as well, but that is between you and your faery friend.

The Singers of the Realms

Of angels, St. Thomas Aquinas wrote, "Angels transcend every religion, every philosophy, every creed. In fact, angels have no religion as we know it . . . their existence precedes every religious system that has ever existed on earth."

These are the great ones, whose wings span the multiverse in all dimensions. They have a multitude of human-given names—angels, devas, gods, dakinis, and many others. It doesn't matter to them what we call them—they just hope we will call *upon* them. They are the Singers of the underlying song of the universe. To the faeries, as to us, they are the Great Ones, the ones who show us, humans and faeries both, what we have the potential to ultimately become. They also help us to move in that direction and comfort us when we fall off the path. We could get very philosophical and complex in discussing them, but we are going to try to keep it simple here, partly because that is the kind of mind I have and partly because each of us is already in our own personal process of learning about them—and that is the important thing.

In Christian theology, angels are the messengers of God. Here we may consider that they are, in a sense, the messengers of Unity (Card 1). They receive the power of Unity, the song of Ekstasis (Card 2), which is brought by the Guardian at the Gate (Card 3) into the world, and they channel it, through their songs, into energies or powers—like love, courage, connection, intuition, and so on.

The Singers are constantly with us, and their energy and compassion are always available. When in need, all we have to do is ask them for help and then be aware of the events and insights that follow our request. When any of the cards in this set are found in a reading, we need to acknowledge the presence of that Singer in our lives, ask for the help it can give us, be open to its guidance, be receptive to the power and energy it offers us, and express our gratitude for its aid.

Thanking the Singers is important *to us* because it completes the circuit, balances the books, and grounds their energy in the physical world so we and others can benefit from it. A gift unacknowledged is a gift neglected and unused. It is through gratitude that we accept their song into our own beings and lives.

When we open ourselves through prayer or meditation or love to the Singers, we allow their essence to flow through us. What happened the last time you prayed for courage or insight or healing or guidance? You will understand much more about each of the Singers if you think of the times that they may have been actively present in your life and what happened then. When you have prayed for courage, how did you feel afterward? Were your feelings or actions any different than they were before your prayer? When we pray for inner strength we get it, although sometimes it comes in a more subtle form than we had hoped for. These personal experiences tell us how the Singers affect our lives. They also give us a sense of how the Singers may interact with other people.

Sometimes the Singers act in our lives very subtly; at other times their presence is almost palpable—intense and clear. The touch of their wings may bring a gentle feeling of strength or love within us, often something that enables us to carry on coping through difficulties. Or we may see miracles, large or small, happen to us or to others. However we experience the Singers (or even if we reject their aid), they are always beside us. In fact, they are within us as well—part of our being, part of the entire universe, part of all that is, was, and will be, the infinite and eternal song of the cosmos.

When we are helped by the Singers, we do not always get what we expect. Sometimes, what we receive may be very unexpected—but it is always what we actually need. This is where trusting the process comes in—a major step in the evolution of individuals.

The Singers are the ministering angels, the great god and goddess, and they are the many faces of Unity, the first to send the Song of Ekstasis to the worlds of Faery and Earth.

The Singers are the givers of grace—that which is given to us whether we deserve it or not, whether we earn it or not, that which is given unconditionally and unstintingly, and which is always available to us when we choose to be open and receptive to it. If any of these appear in a reading, it means that very powerful processes are being worked through, and that we have very powerful assistance with them.

"Keep your eyes and your heart wide open.
Only thus is Faery revealed."
—*Brian*

Card 1 – Unity

Union. Mystical experience.
Spiritual home.

Unity comes first and last. In between we have the illusion of duality, which we all believe in for a very long time. This apparent duality is ultimately shown to be an illusion, but it is an illusion through which we must pass, through which we learn and grow, and then once again return to Unity.

You may have had mystical experiences where you have had true union with other beings or even with the Unity, the One Who Is All. Such experiences change our lives, effectively showing us that the saying "we are all one" is not just a pious belief but is a statement of actual fact. We are not separate like the flowers in a field, but are one. The only way to reach this awareness is to surrender the small everyday self to the larger spiritual self, which *is* Unity. Experiencing full oneness with the Unity is transformative.

Looking at this painting, one observer notes, "All the power is focused *in* here, vast energies. It is as if all that power is looking for a place to happen." This is exactly what is going on. Unity is the energy of the cosmos still unmanifest, still without form. Here we see the dark and the light, masculine and feminine, active and passive, and other polarities, all expressed in balanced, energy-filled, vibrant union. "All That Is is one, and that One is god/dess" is the principle expressed. From this, all else derives. This is the source from which we draw our strength, our very being.

Starter Reading When this card comes up in a reading, it is asking us to remember the mystical concept that we are all one, unified in a holistic universe. It reminds us to look at the needs and goals we have in common with others, and to seek cooperation and community action rather than attempting to do everything on our own. To achieve our goals, we need the active cooperation of others; and to get that cooperation, we must be helpful to them and willing to work with their ideas as well as our own. It suggests that we think of things in terms of equal partnerships rather than in lines of hierarchical authority.

Unity also tells us that we have much to gain by remembering our own wholeness. Resolution of inner conflict is often necessary before we move ahead. It is important at this time that we work toward cooperation and reconciliation, within and without.

Seek the highest good of all involved—and not merely your idea of highest good. Ask for the divine energy of Unity to permeate and guide you.

Reverse We may have become overly focused on the differences and disagreements that seem to separate us from others, and this may be preventing us from achieving our potential for fulfillment and happiness. We may feel alienated, unwanted, and lonely. If this is so, we need to refocus on what we have in common with those around us, far and near. We may need to heal our own attitudes and our beliefs that contribute to these feelings of separation, and we could usefully consider how we might find reconciliation with others. Forgiveness may be a key. Prejudice and judgmental and critical attitudes all push us farther into the delusion of separateness and loneliness.

Move toward allowing others be closer to you, gradually dropping the defensive attitudes that hold them away and keep you alone. Don't wait for others to make the first move toward reconciliation and connection but reach out to them with compassion and selflessness. This may be difficult, even *very* difficult at first, requiring self-study and inner work, possibly with the help of skilled teachers or therapists.

In meditation and prayer, ask to be in communion with the Unity deep within yourself. In Unity there is trust, love, and ecstasy.

Card 2—Ekstasis
Ecstasy. Joy. Rapture. Motivation.

Ekstasis is the song, the energy and power that fills Unity. There is nothing else but that song—no voice to sing, no ears to hear, just the infinite and eternal song, the energy of which completely fills eternity and infinity. This rhapsodic song of bliss is what powers the cosmos and what gives it order and harmony. It is the song that holds the atoms together, the stars in their places, the galaxies in theirs. It keeps our hearts beating, and it is the love and trust that flows through them.

In Unity, there is nothing but the song, the outpouring of undifferentiated energy—the power felt in a mystical experience. The "void" so often spoken of in spiritual literature is not empty, but full—so full that there is no space between one singing and the next. There is nowhere to stand outside of Unity and look at it, marveling.

At the level of this world's reality (and Faery's as well), we have the

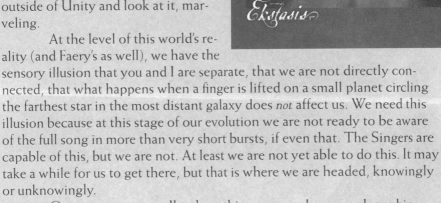

Ekstasis

sensory illusion that you and I are separate, that we are not directly connected, that what happens when a finger is lifted on a small planet circling the farthest star in the most distant galaxy does *not* affect us. We need this illusion because at this stage of our evolution we are not ready to be aware of the full song in more than very short bursts, if even that. The Singers are capable of this, but we are not. At least we are not yet able to do this. It may take a while for us to get there, but that is where we are headed, knowingly or unknowingly.

Our ears are too small to hear this song—only our souls are big enough. The song rings through everything—the wind in the trees, the radiance of distant stars, the beat of a mouse's heart, the rumble of a digestive system, the quiet gurgle of a plant's capillaries, the deep, unheard hum of Earth. Scientists have recently discovered a hitherto unheard part of Earth's song, which is very deep and very slow. Some of them think it may be caused by changing atmospheric pressure, like a gentle, slow patting on a drum. Of course, changes in the atmosphere come primarily from changes in the solar wind and radiation, so, in essence, we see that Earthmother is being gently patted, caressed by Father Sun, and she purrs and hums in response—as do we, her children. Everything is linked; everything is part of the one song, the Ekstasis.

Starter Reading Ecstasy is something people seek. It feels better than good; it feels, well . . . ecstatic. We experience it in tiny bursts and in bigger surges. It enables us to recognize the sacred nature of our own being as an experienced fact, not merely a theory or article of faith. Ecstasy is not something we can make within ourselves, but something that flows through us when we open ourselves to it. It fills us with power and with the motivation to grow, to become what we have the positive potential of being, and to fulfil our purpose in being here and now on this planet. When we are feeling these surges of joy, we are empowered and we know that we are on an appropriate track for us, the track that leads to greater meaning and fulfillment in our lives. This card in a reading says, among other things, go for it! It confirms that we are on course, moving in a good direction, and that we are in harmony with the great song. It says great joy and great accomplishment are within your reach. Its song also lights up and empowers the cards around it, healing the past, intensifying the moment, enlightening the future.

Reverse You may be feeling sorrowful or grieving. Remember that these feelings, too, are a part of the great song. They are a part of love. Don't try to block them; don't try to deny them. Let them flow. If your song is mournful, sing it that way. Let the energy move, let it run freely until it changes. It is important to let ourselves feel what we feel, without denial or blocking, so that we process those feelings naturally, until they transform within us. Only by finding creative expression for such feelings may we complete their process and move beyond them. If life is not going as you wish, *LIVE IT!* Acknowledge it, express it creatively and appropriately, go through it and beyond it. Find the creative balance between wallowing in emotions and denying them. We can accept and gradually transform our feelings. There is a saying, "This too shall pass." It is true about everything—all of our joys and all of our sorrows. Live it and let it pass so that tomorrow can bring you new life, all the deeper and richer for what you have passed through.

Card 3 – The Guardian at the Gate

Passages to new life. Openings. Gatekeeping.

The Guardian at the Gate

The principle task of the Guardian at the Gate is to facilitate the passage from one realm to another and to block the passage of that which is not ready to pass. These realms may be Earth, Faery, the cosmos of the Singers, or Unity. They can also be considered as levels of reality or states of consciousness. In one state of consciousness we are in the ordinary world; in another we are in Faery or Unity. Our bodies don't move but our minds do. The Guardian at the Gate of Unity facilitates the passage of the song into the hearts of the Singers, and aids the passages of humans and faeries into Unity, to be filled by that song when it is their time. We cannot *make* the mystical experience happen to us; we can only open our hearts wider and wider until we are ready, usually only momentarily, to receive it. The Guardian at the Gate recognizes our readiness. Along this line, one man in the Oracle on-line group notes, "We see the energy gathering into the starry gate (or streaming out of it) in the picture, but we cannot tell what is happening on the other side of the gate." This is very suggestive of how these gates and our passages through them can be.

This is the primal spirit of all of the guardians that appear when we are about to step through all metaphorical and most physical gateways. From the guardians of the passages between the worlds to the guardians (doorkeepers) at your own front door, they are all manifestations of one spirit, like facets of different sizes on the surface of one diamond. Naturally, this card shows the Guardian at the gateway to Faery and also to the Faeries' Oracle itself. Every person, every faery, who has ever helped us through an important passage, was manifesting the energy of the Guardian.

Now the Guardian holds the gate of the otherworld open for us. All we need to do is to enter.

Starter Reading Drawing this card indicates that a passage is being made to the beginning of something new in our lives. It speaks of new opportunities and new openings. Passing through this gate may lead to a physical journey, a mental or an emotional one, or a journey of the spirit. It always leads to adventure. This gateway will also lead to significant change in our lives. The passage through such a gate changes us.

The gate we face may not seem like much, the decision to enter may not seem to be a matter of great moment, but the presence of the Guardian at the Gate tells us that something important is happening. It indicates that going forward through that gate is no small thing, but something to be approached with awareness and prayerfulness. We are embarking on a new phase of our lives, and there will be no going back once this gate has been passed. That is the kind of transition the Guardian at the Gate leads us to—always to irrevocable change. We may, of course, ask the Guardian at the Gate for guidance and protection on our journey— and we would be wise to do so.

Alternatively, the presence of the Gatekeeper in a reading may indicate that the querent is being asked to help open a gate for someone else, to help provide an opportunity for them. The job of a gatekeeper (or gatekeeper's assistant) is merely to open the gate, not to push people through it.

Reversed The reversed Guardian at the Gate card can indicate that a gate is closed to us at this time.

Perhaps we are trying to start things that we are not truly ready for—or that are not yet ready for us. Perhaps we are even trying to do something that is inappropriate for us, something that will take us off on a dead-end road. Standing here and banging our heads on a closed gate is not a productive activity.

If we have our hearts set on going in a particular new direction and this card is reversed, a good question to ask is "What do I need to attend to *first* in order to bring this opportunity into my life?" The answer to that might be that unfinished business from the past may make us unready to move on. If so, we need to complete that first, whether it is something in our physical world or in our inner selves.

An alternative possibility is that the gate is open and we are refusing, probably out of fear, to see and enter it. We may be telling ourselves that it isn't a real opportunity, that it wouldn't really work, that we can't (or don't want to) do it after all. We might be feeling both an attraction toward it and a substantial fear of it, and we might be denying the fear and giving ourselves all sorts of reasons and rationalizations and justifications as to why a sensible person would not try that. Yet the gate stands open.

When the Guardian at the Gate appears in a reading reversed, deep thought is required. When it appears right side up and the gate is open wide, prepare for an initiation into a new life.

He of the Fiery Sword

Card 4 —He of the Fiery Sword
The Active Principle. Spiritual will. Justice. Protection.

When the song comes into any of the manifest worlds—this world or Faery or another—it first encounters two principles, sometimes called yin and yang, or masculine and feminine, or Great God and Great Goddess. He of the Fiery Sword is the primary manifestation of the yang principle—action, will, movement, force, fire. We see him in many ways, each one an aspect of his total being. All of the great gods and protectors are aspects of this power.

The fiery sword is the archetype of all magical and mundane swords, and written upon the blade are the words *Draw me not without cause, nor return me without honor.* A member of the Oracle group notes, "His fiery sword illuminates truth and dispels not-truth."

We can call upon the master of the fiery sword when we have difficult things to do, when we need to take action that is going to require much of us, both in will and in compassion. Another of the Oracle group reminds us, "He will do what needs to be done with love."

When looking at this card, my neighbor saw it not as a sword but as a feather of light. He saw it as a symbol of the ability to fly, to rise above things. An Oracle group member saw it as someone reaching up, ascending, surrounded by multiple reflections, and filled with light and power.

To understand this card more fully, please read the comments on She of the Cruach (Card 5). They are the two halves of the same whole.

Starter Reading The presence of the fiery sword's master in a reading can indicate that there is (or there is a need for) clear and focused will and a determination to carry through on decisions, even if much effort is required. Or he can tell us that such will and strength is present in regard to the issues under consideration. We need to consider how he is expressing his will and strength and how that expression may be enhanced or improved.

It is this Singer's energy that enables us to burst the bonds of an outgrown way of being and move on to the next level. He indicates that this is a time to take action based on clear spiritual will. His presence indicates great strength and great potential for good. It also reminds us that, if we call upon him, we will receive assistance. The presence of this card in a reading radiates strength and willpower to the cards around it.

Reverse Like all of the Singers, this card does not have a reversed meaning as such because He of the Fiery Sword is present in full measure throughout the universe on all levels. Reversal here speaks of an archetypal energy blocked or unaccepted by the querent or another involved in the issue. Look to the cards around it to see what may be causing this. When He of the Fiery Sword is reversed, the question we need to ask ourselves is "How may I free strength and will in my life and allow the vital force to flow through?"

"Faeries cannot be pinned down to a page,
a list, a single definition. To grasp their elusive nature
requires direct experience, personal engagement."
                                                                    —*Brian*

Card 5 – She of the Cruach

The Receptive Principle.
Nurturing. Fertility.

She of the Cruach

This is the Great Goddess, the many-named mother of all, and all goddesses are attributes or aspects of her. Her cup, the Cruach, overflows with bounty for all. She is the yin energy of the universe—nurturing, compassionate, and wise. She gives form and brings into manifestation the will and life force of He of the Fiery Sword. *His* is the intention, the action, and *hers* is the manifest reality. In a sense, she is the Cruach holding all the worlds within her being.

One Oracle group member saw the Cruach as a great bowl, like a scrying tool for seeing past, present, or future potential, but filled with energy instead of water. Within it he saw a tower with a moon above it, a farmhouse, and many other bits and pieces of our world. He felt that if you dropped something in the water, these things would scatter out to become reality—archetypes manifesting everywhere. He said, "She is the woman who dreams, and her dreams are the worlds and all that is in them."

Looking at this card, another Oracle group member notes, "What I see here is the energy of being held lovingly in the palm of the hand of the great goddess, followed by a relaxed sigh and release."

She of the Cruach is the holder of all of our sorrows and all of our joys. Her Cruach, the miraculous chalice, is the womb of birth and the cauldron of rebirth, the chalice of healing, the container holding the germinating seed. She is the body, the soul-shrine that holds the spirit and keeps it from being lost or dissipated in a formless fog. She is pattern and form in the abstract and in the specific. Within her we take form, grow, achieve fulfillment, and let go of that form to move on to the next phase of our being.

All of the universe, each individual particle, every being, is cherished by her.

Starter Reading She of the Cruach may indicate a form of pregnancy, a necessary time of nurturing and development. We need to be open to her overflowing grace. She may also indicate a need to allow her nurturing grace to flow through us to others in the form of unconditional love and giving and spiritual healing. She tells us of the need for unconditional receiving, of making the best of what we are offered. She also reminds us that unbounded love and grace is ours, just waiting to be accepted.

The presence of this card in a reading radiates comfort and nurturing to the cards around it.

Reverse Like He of the Fiery Sword and all of the other Singers, she does not have a reversed meaning as such. She fills the universe and is available to all. Reversal here speaks of her archetypal energy blocked or unaccepted by the querent or another involved in the issue. Read the cards around her to begin to understand the cause of this. When She of the Cruach is reversed, the question we need to ask ourselves is "How may I free this energy of acceptance and nurturing in my life and allow it to flow through me?"

Card 6—The Singer of Connection
Spiritual connection. Karma. Balance. Empathy.

This Singer supports all connections, the web of light between all beings, all particles, and between past, present, and future. It brings wholeness to apparent duality and combines all energies, uniting all that was, is, or could be. When we lose awareness of this connection in our lives, we feel isolated, lonely, bereft. Yet the energy is there. We only need to be open to it.

There are emotions that help us open up—love, compassion, trust, and so on. There are other emotions that we tend to close down around unless we make a special effort to keep our hearts open. As you can probably guess, these emotions are feelings such as jealousy, anger, fear, grief, and others of a similarly painful nature. Yet, sometimes, these very emotions, when carried to an extreme, cause us to break down and then break through to the song of Ekstasis. This is a risky way to go as well as an extremely difficult one, because more often the breakdown just stays broken for a long time and then we retreat back to a more crippled version of our original selves.

A far better way to become ever more aware of our essentially holistic nature is to work at keeping our hearts open, seeing relationships, being earthed and centered and connected. In a meditation, someone (and I suspect it was this Singer) asked me to let go of all of my defenses. I argued that surely we needed defenses in this world in order to survive. I was firmly but lovingly told, *"It is only by letting go of all your defenses that you become invulnerable."*

That gave me such a strong shock of recognizing the rightness of it that I couldn't even breathe for a moment. But then, still reluctant (because it sounded like a big job), I muttered that I didn't think I knew how to do that or even what all my defenses were. I was assured kindly that I would receive help if I asked for it. And I know that you will be given the same aid, too.

The Singer of Connection

Starter Reading Through the power of this Singer, all connections are made, held, and released, as appropriate. In a reading, this Singer indicates the connection of things, especially reconnecting those that have been sundered. It is unifying and reunifying. It tells us that we need to be aware of the connections between different aspects of the issue under discussion, as well as the connections between the people linked by it. We also may need to build more connections, a network of mutual support.

The presence of the Singer of Connection in a reading indicates support and strength flowing through the connections between those involved.

Reverse When the Song of the Singer of Connection is dimmed, indicated by reversal, we need to ask ourselves, "Am I earthed? Am I centered? Am I

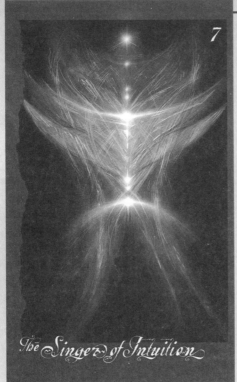

The Singer of Intuition

connected with the source? What do I need to do to be more aware of and enhance my connection in body, mind, and spirit to the universe around me?" There are some suggestions to start with starting on page 181 if you need them.

Card 7—The Singer of Intuition

Perceptiveness. Oracular powers. Awareness. Trust.

The song of the Singer of Intuition carries all of the information there is. Some people believe that this information, often called the *akashic records,* is like a great filing cabinet or library in the sky that we have to go to in order to get information intuitively or psychically. We needn't go anywhere. The Song is sung within our blood and flesh and bones just as it is within the rest of the universe.

If, at humanity's present stage of evolution, we consciously heard the song in all its fullness, we would be overwhelmed, our minds burned out by that energy. A kindly universe has led us to a place in our development where we can consciously hear only bits of the melody. Usually we must develop skill in actively listening for it, but occasionally a few notes resonate so closely with our own being that we become aware of them. These involuntary experiences are what we call hunches or intuition or extended sense perceptions.

We can improve our reception of the song by learning to be very still and to listen in a special way. Later chapters in Part Three give techniques for using this and other oracles as "amplifiers" for the song.

What we get for practicing stillness (through meditation) and listening (just ask and then listen) is the ability to understand and interpret metasymbols, the symbolism beyond the material symbols of oracles and omens themselves. Stars, omens, portents, movement of stars and mice—these are all part of one piece, the one song, and therefore a part of us as we are of them. Understanding them truly is just a matter of learning to be still, to ask, and to listen.

Someday, as we evolve and grow, we will be able to hear more and more of this song and to base our actions and choices on greater knowledge. Patience and practice are the keys to all of the subtle, clear senses—clairaudience (clear hearing), clairvoyance (clear seeing), clairsentience (clear knowing), telepathy (hearing each other without words), precognition (knowing before, glimpses of a probable future).

Starter Reading In a reading, the presence of the Singer of Intuition indicates that information is available to us if we will just listen to our own inner knowing. Perhaps we have already heard it and still doubt our subtle senses. The Singer says this is the time to really listen to our intuition. What are our feelings, hunches, or intuitions about this situation? It is desirable that we should seek solitude, meditate, and practice stillness and patience. This is a time for inward focus, a time to open the inner door to intuition (there are a lot of "in"s in this sentence because important answers are to be found within ourselves).

The presence of this Singer in a card spread radiates special illumination and insight on the other cards around it.

Reverse When the song of this Singer seems especially obscure, as indicated by the card reversed in a reading, we need to ask ourselves, "How can I learn to be more quiet within myself? More peaceful? How can I better listen to the song of knowledge and wisdom?"

*"Not all meanings are meant to be clear at once.
Some ideas take time. Some words are designed to lead us
on inner journeys, with truth hidden deep inside them."*
—Brian

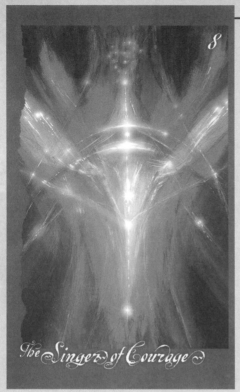

The Singer of Courage

Card 8—The Singer of Courage

Bravery. Sublimation of fear. Moral strength.

Someone once said that courage is not the absence of fear but that which enables us to experience fear and not be stopped by it. It is also what enables us to do what we believe to be right even when there is pressure from others around us to do otherwise. It is what enables us to go ahead into the unknown or the perilous, where there are no guarantees of safety or security.

In our lives we are often, even constantly, confronted with a new world, a new way of being in the world, a new way of seeing and of being seen. Ordinary living takes courage, and to rise above the ordinary into the extraordinary takes even more courage. One of the keys to courage is to consider the fear and find a way to let the *energy* of the fear itself power the action. *That* is true courage.

Often people think of courage as being part of high heroism. It is, but it also has its quiet, hidden side as well—and that may require greater courage because we cannot expect the rewards of praise and approval for it. For example, no courage is needed to be unhappy and self-pitying. We do not need to be self-disciplined or wise for that. However, to open our hearts to the risks and vulnerability of joy and trust requires all of those things, especially courage.

Within each of us, there is the terrified *inner mouse*, and there is the brave *inner hero*. Either part of us can take over from the other. We get to choose which is in charge. The mouse is a magician with only one trick. It can cast an illusion that it is as big as an elephant. Then fear nearly overwhelms us—but we still have choice. Learning to live with and manage the reactive animal within involves transforming emotions like rage and fear into courage through self-discipline and the help of the Singer of Courage.

Starter Reading Most people have decided by the age of three or four what they must do in order to survive. From this decision, this belief about how the world is, most of our fears and self-limitations grow. Have we the courage to discover and break through these limiting beliefs, awaken to greater possibilities, and go for our objectives?

We need to transcend our fears and accept the gift of courage.

Reversed When the Song of Courage has grown faint, and we feel overcome by fear and self-doubt, the questions we need to ask ourselves begin with "What am I *really* afraid of?" Quite often deep soul-searching enables us to discover that our true fears are hidden behind our false fears. It is impossible to face false fears because they are merely shape-shifters and shadows without substance, continually changing form. Facing a real fear is much easier because it doesn't keep changing the rules and moving the goalposts. The question then becomes "What can I do to open my heart to courage so when I feel fear, I can follow through on what I want and need to do?"

As an Oracle group member wisely suggests, another question to ask is "What else is present?" She notes, "When fear of any kind arises in the mind, more space is allowed in the heart if one acknowledges the fear while at the same time looking for whatever else, besides the fear, is also there. Thus one neither ignores nor gives too much focus to the fear itself—and more space opens up within which the fear can be explored and liberated."

> *"Faery wings, formed of shifting light, emotion, and energy, are the manifestation of the power of those beings that transcend the mundane world."*
> —Brian

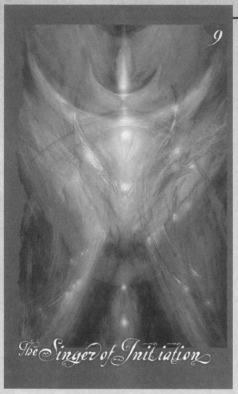
The Singer of Initiation

9

Card 9—The Singer of Initiation

Passage through trial. Triumph. New level.

The Singer of Initiation brings a major transition between old and new. As we prepare to pass through any gate we are greeted by this Singer, who tests us to see if we are ready to enter into the new realm—or whether, for our own safety and well-being, we must stay where we are.

There is no initiation without testing, and this testing must take us to our limits in order to be valid. Initiation is not just a charming ritual with candles and incense and other occult paraphernalia. True initiation is grounded in material reality and it extends through body, mind, and emotions. The testing occurs on all levels of our being. The more profound the change being processed, the more rigorous the test. However, these initiations are only given when the Singer knows we have the potential, the ability, and the opportunity to pass them.

If we pass the initiation this Singer offers, we are strengthened by the process itself. In working through it, we learn something about ourselves, and we move finally and irrevocably from one way of being to another.

Starter Reading Breakthrough. Drawing this card notifies us that significant change and challenge are both occurring in our lives, with the potential for moving into a new realm, which involves a new way of being. This major change has been building for a long time, and the moment is now here to meet this challenge. We may already be aware of the initiation process but perhaps have only seen it as bad luck or fate. It is neither. It is an opportunity to see if we have, deep down, truly learned the lessons we have been working on and are willing to apply them in our lives.

Often, knowing just what the initiation is about can seem one of the most difficult aspects of the process. However, once passed, it eventually will all become clear in hindsight. For now we only need to know, as this Singer said to one Oracle group member, "It can be done—look with your heart."

The presence of the Singer of Initiation in a reading often presages a period of success, of seeing, accepting, and using our own powers at a higher and more ethical level. We move into greater fulfillment of our potentials. It also means taking on a new level of responsibility for ourselves and in the world. The gate is open to us, but we must take the action of stepping through it.

Reversed When we stand in the gateway of an initiation, it is often difficult to tell where we are going, and the process may feel more like loss than like a movement into a new level of being. Prayer for insight helps, but a great deal of the process is about discovering and showing what we can do. This is a test, one requiring much if not all of our inner resources and wisdom. It demands that we go beyond what we have achieved before. Instead of asking things like "Why me?" or "When is this going to end?" try asking, "How can I do this better? How can I handle this more wisely than I ever have before?" Pat's experience with this Singer suggests to her the following questions: "How can I handle this differently, more creatively? Is there another point of view that I have never looked at? What golden door is being offered to me to explore with this apparent problem?"

Card 10 — The Singer of Healing
Healing of body, mind, and spirit.

The song of this Singer has the power of healing deep wounds of the spirit—wounds that can destroy mortals or immortals alike. Faith betrayed, love dishonored, trust abandoned, and other injuries of the spirit all inflict serious wounds, which are reflected in the body's illnesses and injuries. Through the song of healing, we may be restored and renewed, but only if the wounded one is prepared to forgive and let go, returning to love and compassion. As always with all gifts of spirit, healing is offered, not forced, and requires active participation on our part.

True healing must take place on all levels at once—body, mind, and spirit. These levels are inextricably linked, all one piece, and we cannot ex-

The Singer of Healing

pect to change one without changing the others. Our bodies do not do things all on their own. The links between different aspects of being are many, complex, and often obscure. And yet, the *principle* of healing them is simplicity itself. We need only to let go of the things that are hurting us and nurture ourselves with the things that benefit us. So *simple*! So *difficult*!

The song of Healing is present everywhere, and like the other aspects of the great song of Ekstasis, it is without limit. Healing can seem so complex as we dig our way through all our blocks and resistances and old stuff, but in the end it is simply letting go and opening up. Please see page 201 for a little more on healing. Learn everything you can from others; there is a lot of good information out there. Just keep the essential simplicity of the process in mind and you won't go far wrong.

Starter Reading This is the healer's card, and its presence in a reading may speak of healing to be given or of healing to be received. The circumstances and processes of reaching well-being may seem easy or they may bring great challenges. In either case, we are asked to participate in our own healing as we are strengthened by this Singer.

More usually this Singer speaks of both giving and receiving because we cannot truly and freely give without receiving as well. Healing is something that flows through us, not from us, and as such, we are inevitably affected by its passage. Drawing this card tells us of both a need and an opportunity for healing ourselves and perhaps others as well. As Warren, one of my teachers, said, "Healing is not something you *do*—it's something you *are*."

When illness of body, mind, or spirit prevails and we feel disconnected from the great song of healing, the question we need to ask ourselves is "What feelings or ideas or beliefs am I holding on to that keep my wounds open and unhealed?" And, "What can I do to nurture myself and open to the song of Healing?"

Card 11 – The Singer of Transfiguration

Transformation. Transcendence. Metamorphosis.

The Singer of Transfiguration tells us that we have been through the gate, we have passed through the initiation process, and we have reached a new way of being, reflecting deep transformation within ourselves. Things will never again be what they once were.

Things will never be seen in the same way by us, and *this is a good thing!* This Singer's joyful, passionate, bright blaze of color heralds a time of fulfillment and accomplishment.

As with the other Singers, the power and joy of this one radiates especially strongly to the things and beings symbolized by the cards around it. Like the reborn, renewed phoenix, this Singer is aflame with vibrant, expanded life.

There really isn't much I can say about this—not even the faeries seem to have anything to add. They are just sitting around here, smiling blissfully, even ol' G. Doom, and humming an ethereal and beautiful melody. And the cat in my lap, Sylvie, is purring so loudly it sounds like she is singing—as indeed she is. So are we all.

Starter Reading Jackpot! This card in a reading signifies the joy of success after a time of struggle. A new way of life has been accepted and is being integrated. A sense of inner peace is growing. The struggle has all been worth it. This is a time of consolidation and joy, and is both a reward for past achievements and a time of preparation for the next climb up the path.

Reversed Even reversed, this card simply suggests that the realization or completion of this process is just around the corner. Enjoy!

Card 12—**The Singer of the Chalice**
Trust. Joy. Patience. Creativity. Hope. Miracles.

This Singer holds the Chalice from which a rainbow of energies pours like the richest wine. Trust, love, patience—these are things we think of having or not having. We even give ourselves credit for having them, as if we made them ourselves—and yet, they are natural energies of the cosmos, which flow through the Chalice and through us when we are open to them, and flow *around* us when we are blocking them.

People often think that love and hate are two sides of the same emotional coin, but that isn't quite true. Love is not simply the absence of hate; nor is hate the absence of love. They are altogether different things, as can easily be seen. When we are angry, it wears us out and leaves us feeling like less than we were; but when we love, it energizes us, and we feel larger and richer than we were before that burst of love began flowing through us. This is because anger comes from within, burning from our own substance, while love is an energy that flows through us, enlightening and expanding us.

The other energies from this Chalice are also like that. Patience, for example, is not merely the absence of *im*patience. It is a joyful, loving willingness to wait for a process to bring us to where we want to be. It contains trust and love and a special quality of expectant gratitude within it. The same is true of trust—in fact, all of these wonderful feelings are energies that flow through us when we are open to them. They each feel much like the others and, right now, just at this moment as I write this to you, I am being given a glimpse of something wonderful. They really *are* all one thing, something we don't have a word for. We need a word that includes trust and love and compassion and healing and patience and all of the other feelings that enhance and enlighten our being when we allow them to flow through us.

I ask the faeries here if there is a faery name for this rainbow blissful feeling. They nod, smiling, and shrug. I get an unspoken feeling that if you have the feeling you don't need a name, and anyone who hasn't got the feeling isn't going to understand a word for it. It's just one of those things, like the mystical experience of Ekstasis, that we can talk about without understanding or we can understand and not really explain to someone who hasn't already got it. *"So,"* the faeries nod, "get *it!*"

I'd never seen this before but now—just this moment—it is suddenly obvious, as the faeries show me, that this means that we don't have to learn how to open ourselves to each of

12

The Singers of the Chalice

them individually. When we open our hearts and souls to Unity (Card 1), that energy can be focused through so many different lenses of feeling, like white light making rainbows through a prism. If we can learn to be open to any of these Singers, then we can be open to them all if we just remember to. All (I say "all" knowing that it is a mighty *big* all) we have to do is, first, stop doing the things that close us down—let go of the attitudes, beliefs, and emotions that block this energy. Second, we need to actively invite these energies to flow through us—and all that takes is asking. The thing is, the energy is already there. Our asking merely tells our own higher self and the Singers that we, on this conscious level, are ready to accept it. It's like opening your arms to hug someone, or opening a door to let them in.

Although the taste of the contents of this chalice may seem bitter or strange at first, it always leaves a sweet, clean, sparkling taste in the mouth.

Starter Reading With the help of the Singer of the Chalice and of the faeries, you, too, can get this one feeling that is all the good feelings in one—unconditional love, trust, hope, healing, patience, and so on. Open is open. Be open. If you don't know how, ask. It is right there.

Reverse Trust is what enables us to be open to other parts of the song of the Singer of the Chalice. Without enough trust in the process to open our hearts, we close ourselves off from the Singers and the song, decreasing the amount of all those other powers and energies that we allow to flow through us. We can never close off any part of the song entirely, so this tells us that there is always a little bit of courage or hope or whatever that we can find within ourselves and use that as the key to open the door to more. When we perceive the song of this Singer to be muted, its Chalice to be dry, it is only that we need to ask ourselves, "Why not?"; then, don't even try to answer that—just open our heart's door.

Card 13 –Solus
Knowledge. Consciousness. Synthesis. Spiritual empowerment.

Solus stands midway between the realm of the Singers and that of manifest reality—the realms of Faery, this world, and other realms and dimensions. The Singers dwell in a cosmos without boundaries or differentiations, but we and the faeries live in worlds where there are limitations to overcome and boundaries to identify and expand, which helps us to grow.

When we don't know what we need or who to turn to, Solus will help us, if we ask. To an Oracle group member, Solus said, "Allow the surface noise to fade. I'm here waiting."

Solus encourages us to stand on our own feet, to recognize and utilize our own wisdom, to depend on our own strength, and to acknowledge and work with our own good qualities, using them as stepping-stones to improve the less good. Yet, at the same time, Solus recognizes that we cannot do everything alone, and helps us to make the connections and to have the insights that will help us to accept wisdom, energy, and assistance from other realms—especially the realms of the Singers and of Faery.

With faith in the human spirit, Solus sees us as arrows fired from a bow, choosing our own directions and soaring into undreamed-of heights, empowered by trust and the creative life force.

Starter Reading Solus is radiant, energizing, vitalizing. This presence in a reading often indicates that something new is being brought into being in our lives, partly through our own efforts and partly through the help we are receiving from other realms. Miracles may take place. Movement into the light is occurring. This is a time for taking action, passing on our blessings and learning, and for service given from a position of strength.

Reverse When the light and spiritual empowerment of Solus is veiled, we need to remember that this Singer is there to help with seemingly lost causes and forlorn hopes. When you don't even know what to ask for, ask for his help and guidance. And then do the best you can for yourself.

The Sidhe

The Sidhe (pronounced *shee*) are the People of the Hills, the lords and ladies of Faery. They are the Old Ones (even when they are as "young"). All faeries dance, but the Sidhe do so to mediate the powerful energies of the Singers and to bring them into manifestation throughout the worlds. And, of course, for the pure joy of it. Their great alchemical art is the dance of life itself. They are the ones who create, nurture, and build the worlds and their inhabitants, yet they are also available to us individually as guardians, teachers, and comforters. They seem to enjoy creating frequent miracles as well.

*"In one sense, Faery is a land of the past,
where the spirit world and the human
world once worked in closer harmony.
In the faeries' presence, we experience
a nostalgic yearning for that time...
and for all the lost hopes and all the lost
dreams, all that once was or might have
been, and may someday be again."*
—Brian

The Sidhe have sometimes been called gods and goddesses, but that isn't how they think of themselves. They are the elder race, the forerunners, the ancient ones. Once, in the early mists of time, they were as undeveloped as we are now, and we shall eventually, far in the future, be as they are now. Part of our contact with them is to teach us to be more like them and to give us role models for our far future.

In Faery, the concept of lords and ladies is different from what it is for humans. It is not a matter of authority. Imagine telling individual faeries what to do; it would be like trying to herd cats or butterflies—or wasps. Nor is it a matter of having privileges that other faeries don't have. Instead, faery lords and ladies are the most respected of Faery, *for what they do.* They set examples through their work and the way they live. They do not give orders, knowing how important it is to respect the free will of others. Instead, they make suggestions and, more rarely, requests, but there is no force. Therefore we are never punished for disobedience to ungiven instructions, although we may punish ourselves for not cooperating with them by missing out on the wonders we'd have gained if we *had* been more cooperative.

Each of the Sidhe has his or her own potent magic power that acts through all life. The Sidhe themselves are profoundly wise, and their actions are for the highest good of all involved. However, we, too, have those powers in embryo. These abilities are something we gradually *earn* by using them wisely.

These magics sing very powerfully in our lives, and, like the little girl with the curl in the nursery rhyme, when they are good they are very, very good, and when they are bad they are horrid. With these energies, it is important to remember that the flip side of powerful creativity is formidable destruction. The energies channeled by the Singers can only be used by humans creatively for good. Otherwise these energies can be blocked, but never misused. On the other hand, the powers used for good by the Sidhe can be employed by humans either for good or for ill. Such a misuse by humans of the Sidhe's energies always rebounds upon the doer in one way or another. This is just another way of defining karma.

When we humans exercise these powers, we can use them appropriately and compassionately or we can misuse them. The patterns of misuse usually fall into three categories: blocking, twisting, and negating. As we look at each card in the section on the reversed meaning, we will briefly consider each of those difficulties and what we may do about them.

Lastly, although the Sidhe are so powerful and so wise, please do not assume that they are formal or stuffy or pompous. Look at their pictures and consider the company they keep! I have never encountered faeries whose sense of humor didn't sparkle and fizz around them.

Card 14—The Maiden
Auspicious beginnings. Birth. Growth. Joy. Hope.

From her crown of light to her star-jeweled toes, the Maiden is pure joy. She is the face of the force that generates growth throughout all the worlds.

When she smiles, troubles melt. Where she dances, flowers spring from the ground and burst into bloom. It is from the Maiden that the pixies learned the dance that keeps the otherworld turning—and probably our world, too, for that matter. She is newly born every morn, and she carols her plangent song of growth for all beings in all the worlds. She sees the magic and the light in everything and takes endless delight in it.

Yet even though the Maiden is so wonderful and powerful, she is a child and she needs to be cared for, nurtured, and cherished. When she takes the form of a flower, someone must see that she gets enough water and sun. Whenever we look after something new or young, we are caring for the Maiden, whether she is in the form of a blossom, a sapling, a baby, or a new idea. She, in turn, is likely to switch between joyfully and gratefully receiving such nurturing and insisting on an independence that she really isn't ready for yet. She knows, deep within herself, what she needs to

The Maiden

do and become, and she moves toward this with the directness of a child.

The Maiden also has the simplicity and curiosity of a child, seeing with unclouded eyes. She has an openness to life, love, new things, and new experiences. Every moment with her is an adventure, filled with playfulness and hope. Innocent, she is awakening to and learning about the world. Much of her learning comes with laughter and silly jokes, and she trusts what life gives her.

Every time we allow ourselves to be filled with joy, we become more like the Maiden.

Starter Reading The Maiden signifies new beginnings and growth. You couldn't ask for a more auspicious card than this if you are beginning something new. Spontaneity, joy, growth, exhilaration, and promise for the future are signified here. We must note also that, in the early stages of any process, there is vulnerability and a need for protection, shelter, and guidance, but there is also a magical impetus toward burgeoning growth. Trust the process—but take care of the details as well.

The Maiden is also the inner child who needs to be under the supervision of a competent inner adult in order for her to feel secure and loved. She is not happy when we spoil her.

Consider what is growing in your life. Make a list of your hopes, dreams, and plans. Look for the growth within you, and think about how you can cherish and nurture that. Bless the growth you see around you.

Reverse In the Maiden reversed, we find her virtues turned into flaws. When her energy is blocked, we don't allow ourselves to dream, to hope, even to plan a future that is anything but minimal and mundane. We live a cold, sterile, joyless life.

When we twist her energy we become impulsive, unthinking, gullible, lost in dreams that never get translated into reality. There is a tendency to live in fantasy and deny reality, and there is definitely a lack of grounding. Life in a floating soap bubble is perilous—and that is where she is. When living in a dream world has become habitual, the addiction to fantasy is hard to break. It cannot be changed from the outside by others, and even from the inside, there is usually no desire to break through into an unhappy reality until the fantasy world itself becomes too painful to live in any longer.

When the Maiden's energy is seriously reversed, this card can indicate crippling pessimism—an attitude that when possessed means the possessor sees the worst in everything, expects the worst from life, and gets it. Such an attitude creates its own misery and denies one the possibility of joy.

When such a powerful energy as the thrust toward joyful growth is inverted or twisted this way, it is still a powerful energy—and usually requires an equally powerful experience to break free of it. But there is always hope, and those outside the fantasy need to remember that, even while being realistic about the difficulties of changing this state. *Someone* needs to be an adult here.

Card 15 – The Journeyman
Adventure. Independence. Polishing of skills. Travel.

All of the great ones—the saints, the bodhisattvas, and all of those who are filled by the spiritual light—have been on this journey. They went into the wilderness, stepping, like fools, off of the safe paths, into the waiting hands of their gods and goddesses. This is the journey of life, a pilgrimage that begins in ignorant trust, passes through all of the doubts, fears, ups and downs, probably all of the delusions, and certainly all of the confusions. Through it, we learn slowly, painfully, a new kind of trust, a trust in the process, detached from the goal.

Our young Oengus Journeyman, bless him, is stepping out on the journey of life, positively glowing with enthusiasm. Even his toes sparkle. Bright, handsome, and educated, he has completed his apprenticeship in faery crafts and magics, but he has not yet achieved true mastery of his trade. To accomplish this, he must leave the protection of his master and step out onto his path as an independent journeyman craftsman. He is testing himself and his knowledge in the world. He hopes to eventually achieve

The Journeyman

the status of Master Maker (Card 22). Right now, he knows a lot of facts, has all the basic skills, but probably knows less than he thinks he does. He is about to learn about the skills of survival—bartering, persuading, selling, buying wisely, enjoying life, making friends. At least he doesn't need to learn how to iron his own shirts.

Oengus still has lovely, playful, childlike qualities. An Oracle online group member notes that Oengus is playing "Balance the ball on a stick" with the Moon, and adds that he seems to have no constraints, sets no boundaries on what he can do. And because he is magical and doesn't set such limitations on himself, he is able to walk *on* air or water, or *through* the hills, all with the moon nicely balanced both on his stick and in the sky.

Our young Oengus must learn to care for himself. No one is looking over his shoulder to see that he does his work right and eats properly. Oengus may take chances and even make mistakes sometimes, as we all do, but this is how we learn. He is now confronting (and being confronted by) the real world. Here, he will discover that excuses don't buy bread and that the quality and integrity of one's work and actions are what counts, but he has been well taught and pretty well knows this already.

Don't tell him I told you, but Oengus sometimes wears a false moustache, hoping that it makes him look more mature. He has romantic dreams of being a great hero, of becoming *the* supreme master of his craft, and of winning a faery princess. Some of these dreams will come true—perhaps even all of them.

Here we see an innocent being walking trustfully into a situation for which he is not fully prepared (and indeed, cannot be fully prepared) or for which his preparation is as yet untested by reality. He is innocent of previous practical experience of the path he is now treading or the realm of life into which he is moving. This card could be called Innocence Encounters Reality—which is by no means a bad thing.

His faery godmother is lurking somewhere, just out of his sight—as faery godmothers tend to do. Her expression is both gleeful and worried. Her hair is already whiter than it was before he began, and she is keeping her wand fully charged at all times. Although this is *his* journey and he must undertake it himself, almost everyone needs (and is given) a little faery god-mothering from time to time. Good-natured innocence attracts faery guardians; it attracts helpful beings on all planes and in all worlds. It may also attract those who would abuse that innocence; but as long as our intentions are good, our guardians will offer good guidance. We are blessed and cared for—if we allow ourselves to be.

The world is before Oengus with smiles and teeth. Oengus has optimism, cheerfulness, magic skills, and a diligent faery godmother.

Oengus grows within us when we step bravely into the unknown, developing our potentials with hope and optimism and an open heart.

Starter Reading Adventure. Independence. Travel. A long path ahead— we hope. This card speaks to the need to perfect skills in working and living, but it acknowledges having a sound grounding in the basics. Optimistic, innocent, and willing to learn, Oengus also shows us that intuition serves us well—but only if we pay attention to it.

Sometimes, we are operating from theory alone, and our knowledge may or may not be well grounded in reality. This card does not necessarily refer exclusively to beginnings; it can also signify a progression along a path, moving into the unknown from the known, a new phase in an ongoing process. The card may also represent untested concepts or ideas, and suggest a need for balance between the intuitive and the rational as one approaches the unknown.

Consider where you are going. What are your long-term goals? What are you doing that is helping you to move toward them?

Reverse When this energy is blocked, we may feel unable to move forward. There can be two reasons for this. It may be that such a journey is inappropriate at this time and should be delayed until certain conditions are met, *or* it may mean that we are delaying ourselves with our own fear. If you are satisfied that the journey is in the right direction for you, prepare for it carefully and, once you have done so, go for it. Waiting will not make it easier. If it is just fear holding you back, take a long draught from the Chalice of Courage and step out boldly.

Twisted, this energy can involve pretending to ourselves that we are moving forward but in fact, taking a dozen inappropriate paths in order to avoid the one truly right path. The name of the game is *distraction* and *misdirection*—both are a kind of false magic that gets us nowhere.

At its worst, this card reversed can indicate an inappropriate journey, possibly even as undesirable as the path of destruction (for self or others). Consider carefully where you are going here. Consider your major, long-term goals in life and ask yourself how *this* journey helps you to move toward them. Is it perhaps a distraction, a detour, or a fatal stepping off of a cliff? Only we ourselves can decide whether or not we really want to take another step in this direction and why.

Card 16—The Bright Mother
Creativity. Nurturing. Productivity. Intimacy. Sheltering.

She is the Bright Mother of us all and knows that life—all life—is a miracle. The Bright Mother is constantly amazed at its perfection-in-imperfection. She rejoices in its being, sorrows for its growing pains, and exults in its successes. This great lady is both Earthmother and the full, bright Moon, pregnant with the future of all growing things. She feeds us and provides us with air, water, and shelter in an amazing, complex world. She sees to it that we are challenged enough to grow but not so much as to be overwhelmed. If we want more challenges than she provides, we have to give them to ourselves.

The Bright Mother is the guardian of family life, and she creates and holds a nurturing environment for us all. She is the garden where vegetable, fruits, and herbs grow. Thus, she sees and holds the mysteries in ordinary processes of daily life—the bees making honey, the cream turning to butter, the birth of the baby and its growth, the blossom turning to fruit, and the wheat ripening. This lady has loving patience for natural processes, however slow.

Her commitment to us is for life—her eternal life, not our ephemeral in-the-flesh lives. She is present in all of our deep and committed relationships, facilitating nurturing, loving, creativity, and giving. She fosters within us the kind of security that gives us the inner stability we need to explore and adventure out in the world and within our own psyches. She reminds us that there are times when we must put others first because their need is so great, but that in doing so, we must not lose sight of our own needs and nurturing.

One on-line group member sees her keeping an eye on things, making sure that we all do what we need to do. To another she says, "You know me by the joy in your heart and the help in your head. You can have it all—all you have to do is ask." For a third the key word about her is "able—able to carry, care, nurture and enjoy."

One last thing. People tend to project their own experiences with mother and mothering on her. Sometimes this helps us to see her with more clarity, but often it creates muddle. Not all mothers are good and wise. The Bright Mother is.

Each time we perform a compassionate act of nurturing, we become more like the Bright Mother, learning unconditional giving.

The Bright Mother

Starter Reading When the Bright Mother is present in a reading, she speaks of a time of fertility, creativity, and nurturing of ourselves or of others. She might indicate marriage or the birth of a child or a deepening of any kind of a relationship. She also speaks of giving one's all to life, not holding back. She is like a cornucopia, pouring forth abundance. This may be a time to put the needs of others first, taking care of yourself later. Patience may be needed for the process being discussed.

Consider what you have. Acknowledge the people and things in your life—good, bad, and indifferent. This consideration is not to judge, approve, or reject, but merely to recognize what is present in your life. These are your present fulfillments, the things you have created for yourself, drawing upon the power of Unity and the Singers (or not, as the case may be). Once you have looked clearly at what is present in your life, you may want to ask yourself what you want to change.

Reversed These ideas (like the ones mentioned on page 83) apply to men as well as women. They can even apply to institutions such as churches, governments, businesses, charities, and social groups.

When we are blocking the Bright Mother's energy in our lives, we have difficulty giving or receiving nurturing. This may manifest itself physically as well as emotionally. It could mean physical problems such as digestive or eating disorders, or emotional difficulties with giving care or receiving care from others. We may also be unclear about our emotional boundaries.

When her energy is twisted, we see the "smother mother" who refuses to let those within her care grow up and become independent, crippling them in their adult life. Or perhaps the warped energy becomes the "martyr mother" who "sacrifices everything for you" (whether you want it or not) and then expects you to sacrifice everything for her forever. If we find in ourselves tendencies to do these things, we need to change both our habits and our deep programing, which may require professional help.

At worst, the Bright Mother's energy becomes a fire of destruction, creating burnout where there should be nurturing. This happens when we give until we are exhausted and don't take time to nurture ourselves or allow others to do so. Rage or cruelty directed at those who rightfully depend upon us also falls into this extreme category.

Card 17—Himself
Natural law. Life force. Magic. Shamanic power.

Known as Himself, this Sidhe is guardian of both the hunter and the hunted—and finds no conflict in that because he understands the many necessary balances of nature. The living bond between all life, Himself is the breath that moves, the atom that dances, and his magic is in pure being—living, loving. Oengus Journeyman and the Master Maker have the magic of doing, of the creation of things. The Bright Mother has the magic of manifesting and nurturing, but Himself—he has the magic of procreation, of dancing the spark of life into being. His presence brings magic and life into a world where it is shaped and given form by Earthmother. He dances as the Bright Mother gives us birth, powering us into the world. He is the Great Father.

At the other end of our lives, he is the one who dances the great dance of life and death, and it is Himself who, when the Piper (Card 24) plays his lonely call on the wave-swept shore at year's end, dances open the gate between the worlds so that the dead may pass beyond. It is also he who is willing to sacrifice himself, when that is necessary, for the sake of those whom he protects.

Himself

In between those two extremes, his wild yang energy is channeled through humans to benefit tribe and family. His family is all of us, human and animal. Shamans draw upon his power, and the best healers channel a balance between his power and the Bright Mother's nurturing energy.

Even as our hearts beat within us, we learn to mediate the life force through joyful being and action. Expressing this power through healing and love and trust, we become more like Himself.

Starter Reading When Himself appears in a card spread, he not only indicates that a great amount of energy is present in the reading, but he also strongly energizes the faery cards around him. Everything he touches becomes *more* of whatever it is—more alive, more vigorous, more powerful, more awesome, or more awful. This card in a reading can indicate great vitality, victory, or triumph, confidence, and power. There is leadership, an ability to command, steadfastness, and integrity—wild power held and channeled for the good of all by will.

Himself speaks of protection, either of the querent or of someone the querent owes protection to, like a child or an elder. Acceptance of paternal responsibility is important, as are deep and committed relationships. He is the preserver of the natural world and its balances.

Shamanic power may be indicated here, as well as a potential for powerful spiritual healing. This card may also speak of erotic energy, passion, and potent creativity.

Reversed When the energy of Himself is being blocked, we feel limp, enervated, drained. There may also be depression, either physical or emotional. Energy may be locked into obsessions or may swing from blocked to out of control.

Twisted, the life force, strength, and/or authority may be being misused as arrogant aggressiveness or violence toward others. When this card is reversed in a reading, careful and prayerful consideration needs to be given to how the energy can be rechanneled into its naturally creative and protective mode.

At worst, this potent energy becomes a force for war, oppression, and domination. The very worst is when brutality or twisted sexuality is turned on the very persons this energy within us should be protecting. As in all the Sidhe powers, what has great potential for good can also have great potential for destruction. Volcanic release may occur.

Card 18—The Lady of the Harvest
Completion. Grief. Loss. Harvest. Release.

After we have experienced the nurturing and fulfillment of the Bright Mother, the Lady of the Harvest, also called the Old Woman or Crone, helps us to let go of what is finished and liberate ourselves to move on to the next phase of our activities and relationships. As in the natural world, the old becomes compost for new growth in our lives. The Lady helps us to adapt to change and release.

Often we associate the Lady of the Harvest with loss, regret, and grief—and often we are right to do so. The basic phases of grief are shock/denial, anger/guilt, emotional storm, acceptance, regaining of perspective, the beginning of healing, and the deepening of our capacity for love. The Lady of the Harvest understands grief and is patient and kind as we go through the sometimes painful process of letting go. We may well need to be patient and kind with ourselves.

We should note here that the grieving process is the same for little losses and large ones; only the time scale and the intensity of the emotions vary, but they vary enormously. We might go through all the grieving stages of a small loss in a few minutes while it may take years for a greater loss.

On the other side of this letting-go business, there are many things that make us lighter and happier when we release them—old traumas, tasks, or stages in our lives that we are glad to have finished, unhappy relationships, or feelings that cause us pain and inhibit our growth. Sometimes we simply comfortably finish with one aspect of our lives and move on to the next, happily anticipated one. Such releases are cause for celebration, and the Old Woman joyfully celebrates with us. In this card we see both the patient acceptance of loss and the joyful celebration of liberation.

When we liberate something in ourselves or in the world, we grow to be more like the Lady of the Harvest, developing her capacities within us.

Starter Reading It is time to accept change, to move on to the next phase. Power and strength in the present and future come from releasing the past. This is a time of liberation, and we might as well cooperate with it. It will happen, whether we want it to or not. Release and liberation may be painful or joyful, depending on the circumstances. Cry if you need to, be joyful if that is appropriate, but in either case trust the process, acknowledge what you feel, and prepare to move on.

Reverse When we block the liberating energy of the Lady, we may refuse to accept a loss or cling to outgrown pains, traumas, or limiting ideas. We may deny reality. Shock and denial are the first stage of grief, but we need to move on past that to eventually gain a healthy balance in the present. If we stay in denial, the grief cannot heal. Denial can be the denial of reality or the denial of our feelings. Either one prevents us from moving on to healing. The universe moves on; we have no choice really but to move on with it.

Twisted, the energy of release can move in various directions. One possibility can be the "letting-go program," an automatic process like a computer program, where we compulsively push away things we actually want and need. Another twist on this is to turn away from the things in our lives that give us satisfaction, fulfillment, or joy because we cannot have the one thing we want—so it seems reasonable to have nothing at all. This kind of sulking can easily be carried to an extreme.

The destructive mode of release can be summarized by the bumper sticker saying: *If you love something, let it go. If it doesn't come back, hunt it down and kill it.* This is the "if I can't have it, no one will" attitude. From the outside, such attitudes seem obviously stupid and selfish, but to someone caught in one of the less rational stages of the grieving process, they may seem the only solution—a solution that is not a solution to anything at all.

Card 19 — The Sage
Wisdom. Hidden knowledge. Retreat. Old age. Patience.

The Sage is also the shaman. Not all wise men are shamans and not all shamans are wise men, but this one is both—power informed by wisdom and wisdom made manifest by power. This is also the face of Father Time, and we see the colors of the seasons surrounding him. Sometimes, he is Old Man of the Mountain, the hermit who searches within for wisdom and understanding, and then is willing to share it with any true seeker who comes to him.

His "blind" eye enables him to look into other worlds, other realms, and the wisdom buried deeply within each of us, where the Singers dwell. He has reached a stage of life where he has let go of many of the activities of younger beings, retreated somewhat from the outer world of Faery, and has become more deeply immersed in the inner landscapes of knowledge, inner vision, contemplation, and spirit. On the exterior, he lives simply, almost austerely, but his inner world is filled to overflowing with richness.

In order to pursue his studies more thoroughly, the Sage has cultivated detachment. Some may see this as remoteness or coldness, but he is no less loving for that. The Sage finds the inner connections between everything. He sees the connections, relationships, and consequences between seemingly separate ideas, beings, and things.

Love and compassion are the inevitable consequences of seeing truly, and this leads the Sage to share his learning with others. Like any other wise elder, he leads by gently teaching from his vast store of wisdom. When asked for his judgment about something, he is discriminating and generous-hearted. He turns a blind eye to punishment, feeling that what is needed is mercy and a way of teaching those who err so they will not make the same mistakes again.

The Sage is constantly learning. While on the one hand he values tradition and stability, he also understands and values the need for growth and change. He can't go for a walk or a flight around the neighborhood without discovering something new and trying to see how it fits into the whole. He is always expanding his understanding of reality and deepening his awareness.

As we develop patience and compassion intertwined, we begin to manifest the wisdom of the Sage.

Starter Reading Here we see wisdom and deep inner understanding. One of the keys of wisdom is to organize, integrate, and simplify one's thoughts. Complexity often leads to confusion; simplicity is to be valued. This card signifies mental discipline informed by balanced learning and compassion. Tradition is valued but appropriate change is accepted. The Sage knows when to let go and when to move on. He knows when to retreat and think things over. He compassionately and wisely shares his knowledge with others, teaching by example as well as by precept. The scales of justice are balanced in the Sage's hands. This card in a reading also signifies the need for deep consideration and refined judgment applied with compassion and mercy.

Reversed When the wisdom of the Sage is blocked, artificial or inappropriate boundaries are set between different aspects of life. We become unable to apply learning in one sphere to other aspects of life. Or information is withheld, kept secret when it could benefit others, which in turn would benefit us. Sometimes learning is blocked by the belief that we already

The Dark Lady

have all the answers, but we never actually do.

Twisted, the Sage's accumulation of facts and information becomes unwisdom—knowledge misused and distorted, facts distorted for selfish purposes, information used to the detriment of others. There is always a risk of this when we set out to *prove* something rather than to *discover* something. Other twists include being excessively critical, being cold and uncaring, or being cynical or embittered. These are all faults of balance.

At its worst, knowledge and experience are channeled toward the destruction of the self or others.

Card 20 – The Dark Lady
Unconscious power and wisdom.
Rituals. Mysteries. Secrets.

The Dark Lady is the high priestess of the Mysteries. She understands how to surrender to divine power, to Unity (Card 1). She has the profound, intuitive knowledge that is only to be found by looking deeply into our own beings and natures. We find her through meditation, in sleep, and within inner peace, ecstasy, and total despair. I am writing this at the time of the dark moon, which is her time.

She is the guardian of beings unborn, of unconscious ideas, and of seeds sprouting in the dark, cold earth, tender and fragile and as yet unready to face the bright sun and the winds of spring. She holds the embryonic hopes we have not yet realized we have.

The Dark Lady is the mistress of spiritual ritual. The purpose of a ritual is not the power it allegedly has over gods or spirits or faeries, but the very real power it may have over us, putting us into a state of consciousness where we may better connect to our own magic and to otherworld beings. The Dark Lady understands that ritual is something we surrender to and we allow to enfold us, rather than something we do or control.

When we have been through a living cycle—birth and growth with the Maiden, nurturing and fulfillment with the Bright Mother, releasing and letting go with the Lady of the Harvest—it is the Dark Lady who passes with us through the night of endings and death, whether of the body or of the soul or simply of something passing through our lives. It is she who holds and guides us as we reconceive ourselves and prepare to be born anew. In as simple an act as breathing, we see all four of them—inhaling with the Maiden, the moment of fullness with the Bright Mother, exhaling with the Lady of the Harvest, and the moment of empty, waiting stillness with the Dark Lady.

She is there in our very last moments of deepest grief, helping us to move forward to the stillness and peace of the place beyond grief. Our sorrows are transformed within her. She teaches us surrender, walking with us through the valley of the darkest shadow. She is there as we experience the ecstasy of release. Then she guides us back to this reality, renewed and illuminated. From her come those spiritual awakenings that seem to blossom within us out of nowhere.

When we travel through the darkness, inner or outer, we learn the strengths of the Dark Lady.

Starter Reading We may reach the realm of the Dark Lady through grief, through deep surrender, through ecstasy, or through profound ritual. This card in a reading suggests that it is time to withdraw from the ordinary world to revitalize ourselves through retreat and surrender to the source, Unity and the song of Ekstasis. This is a time of preparation for rebirth, of restoration and regeneration. What is hidden is getting ready to be revealed. Celebrate this passage through the unknown, rich, fertile, hidden realms of the Dark Lady.

This is the time in the natural cycle of life when we open ourselves to and receive the inflowing energies of Himself (Card 17), when we become power-full, overflowing with the life force. It may also be a time of prophecy, magic, and foretelling of the potentials of the future—a time of self-awareness, self-knowledge, and encounters with the hidden worlds. Meditate, retreat, seek serenity and inner peace.

Reversed When we block the Dark Lady, we may be frenetically active, occupying ourselves with the outer world and ignoring the call of the world within. We may be resisting profound change and renewal. In order to keep our feelings repressed and hidden from ourselves, we may become aloof, cold, and inaccessible, holding back from others as a way of holding back from ourselves.

When we twist her living process within us, we may experience sexual blocks or frigidity or impotence or some other form of disability in making connection with others and with the source of being.

At worst, we use the magic of the inner realms for the purposes of destruction or manipulation, becoming black magicians. If we choose to do this, which is the closest thing the faeries know to an unforgivable sin, we may harm others, and we shall certainly do very serious damage to ourselves.

Card 21 — The Faery Who Was Kissed by the Pixies
Love given. Love received. Metaphorical open-heart surgery.

Pixie kisses are not chocolate like the well-known Hershey's Kisses, but the Pixies claim that they are a whole lot sweeter and don't do anything dreadful to your teeth. However, if the pixies have been munching faery chocolate, some pixie kisses give people freckles. As Brian wrote, "The pixies say that there cannot be too much kissing! A faery kiss is a blessing indeed." Pay attention when you feel a faery touch on your cheek or lips. Pixie kisses (in fact, all faery kisses) are to be noticed and savored. If you do notice, you will find yourself smiling without meaning to, and feel a surge of warmth swell in your heart.

This faery, Morna, is the queen of love—all kinds of love: brotherly, sisterly, parental, friendly, unconditional or conditional, either or both. She tells us, *"It takes perfect people to have a perfect love. But we, imperfect as we all are, may have many loves—each one perfect for who we are and for what we need now. These loves may not feel perfect, they may not look perfect from the outside, but they fit us now. If we don't like them"*—she shrugs—*"then we need to change ourselves so that a different kind of perfection fits us."*

Here we see Morna in her role as heart surgeon, using the power of love to help us open our hearts when we have closed them out of fear, helping us to expand and become more of what we have the potential to be. Yes, it is true—having an open heart, being willing to love and be loved, makes us vulnerable to loss and grief. But Morna assures me (and I believe her) that once a heart is truly and fully open, even the deepest grief becomes bittersweet, like dark chocolate, and there is no pain that is not balanced by the greater joy of love.

The feeling of *giving* love is what makes us feel good. What keeps us from enjoying it fully is our desires to own others and to have them constantly "prove" our importance to them. Such proof is impossible. However, this kind of conditional and self-limited love is part of how we learn about real love. If ever you hear yourself asking, "Do you really love me?" or saying, "I don't think you really love me," then you know that the love *you* are giving to the other is conditional and limited.

Morna would like to help us learn to love others without conditions, and she also would like us to learn to love while still staying properly centered within ourselves. It is

The Faery Who Was Kissed by the Pixies

important for us not to lose ourselves in others and let their desires become ours while losing sight of what we need for fulfillment in our own lives. In the long run (or even in the not-so-very-long run) that never works out. We only *think* we know what others want and need, and sooner or later we get it disastrously wrong—usually by thinking we know what they *ought* to need. We are all learning about love, and in the process of learning, we all act as teachers for each other. Ram Dass said, "The karma of relationships is the hardest karma there is."

"Believe it!" Morna advises. And this is true, no matter what the relationship is. But for all that, love in its purest sense is the fast track to self-realization and enlightenment. The Wild Thing at the top of the picture is filled with bliss and is longing to cuddle its way to enlightenment. Remember, everything and everyone in Faery glows with its own light. So do we. Much of that light is the glow of love. Remembering that is important.

Opening our hearts more widely to the giving and receiving of love evokes the well-kissed Faery within.

Starter Reading *Oh, wow!* What can I say here? Love, sweet love. Accept it, burnish it up, add to it, and pass it on.

The presence of the Faery Who Was Kissed by the Pixies suggests giving and receiving love and intimacy in any of a wide variety of relationships. She gives notice that this is a time to open and heal our hearts. Different aspects of life may well be flowing happily together, healing separations and hurts from the past. Bonding may take place and deep feeling emerge. Changes for the better may occur in all aspects of life, but especially in relationships, which may be deepening and becoming richer. You may be experiencing love therapy for opening the heart as new relationships begin and old ones develop. Enjoy!

Reverse When we block love, obviously we refuse to give or receive it. An interesting thing here is that love is an energy, an aspect of the life force, and it flows through us whether we admit it or not. The unhappy souls who refuse to acknowledge it still have it within them, ignored, denied. Another way we block love is to become the kind of people pleaser who wants to do everything for others but won't let them give in return.

The twisted energy of love shows up as jealousy, possessiveness, attention-seeking, and demanding behavior. It is focused on getting rather than giving and results in unhappiness rather than happiness. It is also based on the entirely false idea that there is not enough love in the world for everyone to have as much as they need. Another twist is believing that it is up to others to make us happy, when really this is our own responsibility.

One of the worst things we can do is to deny love—to pretend we feel it when we don't and to pretend we don't when we do. Another is to try to destroy love between others by any means for any reason whatsoever. And the worst of all is taking advantage of the love of others to betray them.

"Faeries are both luminous and illuminating."
—Brian

Card 22 – The Master Maker

Skill, Craftsmanship. Magician. Moral strength. Invention.

The Master Maker is the master of the forge, upon which we create our futures and forge our own souls. He sees the world beyond the otherworld, the world of first causes. Through his magic, he brings them into his own world of Faery. From his world, these concepts trickle down into our own, through dreams and visions picked up by artists and craftsmen everywhere. But he makes the first, the original. He is the great inventor, and the sign above his door reads: *Practical Problems Solved Here.*

He sings as he works and, as in all faery magic, his song does as much to shape objects as do the blows of his hammer. Healing cups, magic swords, faery jewels, crowns of stars, and other bespelled works of the finest craftsmanship pass through his forge and beneath his hammer. The master of fire, air, earth, and water, he adds the faery element of moonlight to everything he creates. He would be the first to tell you that superb craftsmanship, however magical, is hard work— joyful and energizing hard work, but always challenging. As the Master Maker reminds us, *"No job is too small to do beautifully."* His work is done as well as possible, even where it will never be seen by anyone else.

Bringing ideas into excellently crafted reality can only be done when we, like the Master Maker, are willing to plan meticulously, begin carefully, and persevere through difficulties, learning still more of our craft as we work. Craftsmanship is also a labor of love. We must be willing to tackle difficult challenges and have a determination to surpass previous achievements. Patience is always required, as is the willingness to do a thing again and again until it is even better than the best one can do. The Master Maker has the moral strength to refuse the temptation to do anything less, and he is a protector and teacher of the traditional values of his craft. Yet, in balance to all of this, the Master reminds us that we also need to learn our own limits—not everyone can do everything superbly. When we discover our talents and choose our craft, *then* we gain great joy and fulfillment from developing that skill into an art.

We grow more like the Master Maker each time we do the best we can—and then stretch ourselves to do a little better than that.

Starter Reading Do whatever you do as well as you can. And then make it even better. The Master Maker reminds us that our very best work is *always* desirable, and in the present situation, it is necessary for success. In fact, he asks that we surpass our previous best. Don't cut corners and don't take the easy way. Whether making a thing or fulfilling a concept, be sure the design is elegant, pure, and functional, and then follow it, attending to every detail in its turn. He says, *"Design beyond your skill, and then raise the level of your skill to fulfill it."* Give and accept only the best, and do it with love of your craft, whatever that craft may be.

This card speaks of long-lasting achievement, creative problem solving, and confident action. It may suggest cooperation with others, especially from a position of responsibility, or of teaching one's craft to others. Success comes from practical application of traditional principles, in life and in work

Reversed When the Master Maker's wisdom and skill are blocked, shoddy craftsmanship is a problem. It doesn't matter what the art or skill or craft is, it doesn't matter whether it is physical or intellectual, this situation is likely to deteriorate badly if people do not give their best—and then do even better than that. This card reversed may represent haphazard work, mediocrity, lack of skill, or unrealized potential. While traditional values of quality and integrity of workmanship are important, being dogmatic or stuck in outworn ways just for the sake of tradition is another block to the art of the craftsman.

Twisted, the wisdom of this card becomes indicative of the misuse of craftsmanship. For example, we might use our skills in finishing to hide flaws in a structure of either a physical object or a concept or organization.

The destructive mode here is to use our skills and craftsmanship, in any field, to create the means of destruction, whether of lives or the environment or hopes and dreams.

Card 23—The Green Woman

Wildness. Natural magic. Expectant gratitude. Untrammeled creativity

The Green Woman dances naked in the moonlight—and in the sunlight and the shadows as well. She doesn't care what you think of her; she knows her own worth from her experience of life. She is the feminine vital vegetative force that enables a root to crack stone, the reed to bend in the wind, and the oak to stand against the storm.

The Green Woman

The graceful, slow-motion dance of the Green Woman shows us how to release the constraints of artificial rules and limitations and find our true pattern of growth. Each of us, rooted or not, has an inborn pattern of perfection to guide our growth. Earth-mother nurtures us, Sunfather energizes us. Storms batter us and sometimes we must bend before them. Other life preys upon us on the one hand and nourishes and supports us on the other. Within the framework of the real world, we seek our path to realizing our own potential and finding our own fulfillment.

The Green Woman reminds us that where the ground is fertile, *something* will grow. It may be nettles or thistles or roses or carrots or sand burrs or peaches, but it will be something because fertile earth never remains empty. She tells us to stay earthed, to attend to our own growing ground, keeping it fertile, aerated, and well watered—and to pay attention to what grows there. It is up to us to root out what we don't want within ourselves and to nurture what we do.

She also reminds us to count our blessings and deal with our difficulties. A tree grows where the seed falls, as do all of our rooted brothers and sisters. They teach us of the importance of making the best of what comes to us, showing patience and perseverance in adversity. When a plant is thirsty, it can only do limited things to assuage its thirst, like slowly driving its roots deeper in search of water, but mostly it must wait for water to come to it. Although we have legs and can often take action to get what we want (or at least try to), there are some things beyond our reach. These are the things we can learn from the Green Woman's example, waiting patiently and with expectant gratitude.

Yet, at the same time, she counsels us to take risks, to let new and unfamiliar wild seeds grow and see what they may become. Watch them closely—some of them may be miracles waiting to happen in our lives.

As we develop our own free and untrammeled creativity, the Green Woman grows within us.

Starter Reading The Green Woman speaks to us of caring for our growing ground and of the physical satisfaction of being our natural selves and practicing our own innate magic. This is a time for enhancing the growth of our talents and abilities, a time of blossoming that will bear fruit.

It may also be a time of growing maturity and self-confidence. Experience trusting yourself and trusting the process of growth.

She also reminds us of material reward ahead, the harvest of the seeds we have planted and nurtured. She counsels boldness and perseverance in the face of adversity, yet she also reminds us that sometimes the only action we can take is to wait patiently and keep growing.

Reverse When her energy is blocked, growth is stunted.

Twisted, the energy of growth goes awry, and we move in directions that are either dead ends or simply inappropriate for us. Or perhaps we try to shift from one extreme to another, between growth and stasis, which only yields twisted, stunted, and warped results.

In its destructive mode, the energy of growth goes wild. Cancers, both physical and emotional, may result. Alternatively, there may be no growth at all, but in Faery and this world both we must either grow or die. We cannot simply hold still.

Card 24—The Piper
Music. Order. Harmony. Seduction. Empathy.

The secret melody of the Piper drifts through our lives, offering us a means to communicate from the heart and without words. His music conveys our emotions to one another, emotions that are audible only in the listening ear of our hearts. His approach to us is gentle and wordless. He may send us his melody through the whisper of leaves, the rustle of grass, the song of a bird, the hum of city traffic, the buzz of a refrigerator, or the whirr of a computer. He asks that we listen to the world around us, especially to the unspoken words of others, humans and faeries, plants and trees.

The Piper

Among the other things the Piper offers us is the ability to bring him our sorrows and pain in the form of music so that he may help us to heal them. Sing a sad song to this faery and he will add to it the energy of cleansing and healing, if we are open to healing. His natural music also offers us tranquility, if we take the time to be still and listen to it.

The Piper's music can be seductive and attractive—even magnetic. He lures us with our own daydreams. Sometimes, we allow the music of the Piper to enthrall us into illusion, especially the illusion of control over that which we cannot control. However, if we use that illusion (our own self-deceit) to break through into greater truth, it has served its real purpose.

He calls to us, asking that we listen—listen to him, to the faeries, to each other's hearts. His piping may seem elusive, hard to hear, diffused, yet it is very clear and it brings us the meaning of our lives.

Working on developing more order, harmony, and beauty in your life? Then you are singing to the tune of the Piper—and becoming more like him as you do.

Starter Reading To get what you want, the Piper recommends that you try polite requests and gentle, patient persuasion—and then wait, quietly welcoming, for it to come to you. Seek harmony and tranquility in yourself and in the world around you. Use tenderness and gentleness. This card speaks of a time of harmony, creativity, and increasing order. It tells of communication without words—the music of empathy and the awareness of the feelings and concerns of others. This is a time to pay attention to the subtlety of others' expressions of feelings and ideas. Look past the surface and listen as you would to a beguiling melody on the very edge of hearing. He also plays melodies in our dreams, which may be filled with meaning and importance, and then he leaves it up to us to understand what they mean.

This may also be a good time to be aware that others may be listening to us with sensitivity and clarity—so much so that they may hear what we are truly saying more clearly than we do ourselves.

This card may also signify musical talent or ability, or it may be suggesting that the use of music is in some way important at the present time.

Reverse When we have blocked out the melody of the Piper we can be like someone mesmerized, lost in a dream, stagnating. Alternatively, this card may represent people so vague and diffused that they are insufficiently earthed to be able to keep commitments—or even to remember that they have made them and it wasn't just another fantasy. Self-absorption, moodiness, and self-deceit can be problems. Altogether, unreliability and untrustworthiness are a real problem. Look at the other cards to see if anything can be done to rectify this or if you just have to take this into account and make your plans accordingly.

When the power of the Piper is twisted, it becomes manipulative and may be aimed at seducing others into something against their judgment or ethics. It becomes like a spider waiting at the center of a web to entrap someone.

One of the worst abuses of this energy is to use our empathic understanding of the needs, hopes, and dreams of others to attempt to lure them into self-destructive ways, especially by playing on their illusions, delusions, and confusions.

Card 25—The Faery Godmother
Gifts. Talents. Grace. Helpful lessons.

One morning recently, I was having breakfast at the local café and my favorite waitress, Peggy, stopped by my table and asked what I was working on. I showed her my scribbled-in copy of *Good Faeries/Bad Faeries* and explained that I was "choosing" the cards for an oracle deck. (Of course, the faeries were choosing them, but I didn't necessarily want to explain that to the whole café.) Peggy had been having a bad morning with difficult customers, and she had reached the stress point where she was dropping and spilling things, which only made matters worse. I encouraged her to pause for a bit, since the café wasn't really busy, and take a look at the faery pictures. She thought she couldn't, but I employed the Piper's wiles (Card 24) of friendly coaxing, and she took a little time out to look.

The Faery Godmother

When Peggy got to the page of the Faery Godmother, she stopped and smiled. "Oh, *yes!*" she said. "*She* must be in the deck. Definitely she *must.*" The longer Peggy looked at her, the bigger her smile grew, and the more insistent she was that I include Sairie in the deck. When she went back to work, I noticed that she still had a little smile on her face and her whole energy had changed. Things were not jumping out of her hands any longer, either.

This is how Sairie the Faery Godmother works. She gives us grace to help us along our way. It might be a little touch of faery dust to lift a mood, it might be a conspicuous miracle, it might be anything in between. She protects us from the ill will and plain stupidity of others and from our own mistakes. She untangles the snarls in our psyches and bestows gifts upon us—whatever she feels we need. Sometimes she gives us choices when we thought we had none.

Grace is the good fortune we get from the universe even when we don't deserve it. In fact, deserving or not deserving is not the issue. We *are*—and therefore, we are loved. It's that simple. Sairie the Faerie Godmother is a giver of grace, and occasionally (quite often, in fact) of useful lessons. She tries not to interfere with our learning processes, but she adds that little touch of faery grace that helps us to learn a little faster sometimes. Quite often she acts in our lives through the hands and hearts of others.

The Faery Godmother is the only one to wear a crown of stars, flowers, and branches, which says a lot about her. Luckily, each of us has a faery godmother to provide the extras that our guardian angels are often too busy to think about.

Faery godmothers in general are well known for their love of parties. Don't forget to invite them to your festivities and special occasions.

The Faery Godmother glows through us as we perform loving and appropriate kindnesses for others and develop our capacity for unconditional love.

Starter Reading   Sairie offers last-minute rescues. When she turns up in our readings, good things may well be happening that we don't think we deserve—or that we do deserve but haven't thought to ask for. Almost imperceptibly she teaches us about giving and receiving unconditionally, helping us to open our hearts to love and acceptance. She sometimes showers us with abundance. Keep an eye out for unexpected good fortune, especially when you thought you saw bad luck headed your way.

Remember to say thank you by passing a kindness on to someone else. Practice a little faery godmothering yourself and see how enjoyable it is. Part of the fun of it is to do it so that the recipient doesn't know where the gift came from.

Reverse   When we block the Faery Godmother from our daily lives, things are harder than they need be. When we attempt to live without the grace of the faeries and of heaven, life is an uphill struggle.

When we twist this energy, we become judgmental and get tied in knots trying to decide who is "worthy" and who is not. We tie strings to everything we offer others—and then we trip over them.

At worst, we sour our lives, sharing nothing and taking from others—becoming the selfish, greedy thief in the night instead of the sparkling Faery Godmother, who glows with the light from within. No matter how much that thief accumulates, he will never have enough to feel happy or secure or loved.

Card 26 – O! That Gnome

**Trickster. Creative chaos.
Wild gifts. Breaking habits and
patterns.**

This is the Trickster, who exists in
every world. He comes to us wearing
our own faces to fool us into thinking
that his ideas are our own. He brings
creative chaos into our lives. He helps
us break down old habits by showing
us how silly they are. He encourages
us to fall on our faces so that we get a
different point of view, looking up
past our mud-smeared noses. He helps
us get ourselves into situations in
which we discover gifts we never
knew we had—often because there is
no other way out of the mess we got
ourselves into.

O! That Gnome

As Brian mentions, *That*
Gnome is unreliable and sometimes
encourages drunkenness. This is true . . . he certainly doesn't always do as
we expect—but our expectations are our problem, not his, he says. As for
drunkenness, *in vino veritas* (in wine, there is truth). When we let down our
mental censors and filters, we sometimes come up with discoveries about
who we really are and what we really want that we hadn't let ourselves
know. When he appears, it is breakthrough time, and all too often, the first
step in breakthrough feels just like breakdown. There *are* better ways of
doing this than getting drunk or going through a psychotic break, but the
better ways take skill, and he has to work with what he has—us, just as
we are.

"*That* Gnome tells wild and wonderful long-winded stories, complete with demonstrations of the action and much arm waving," an on-line
group member says. He adds, "*That* Gnome is full of knowledge, but the
trick is sorting out the truth from the fiction. It takes a lot of good sense to
be able to listen to him. He isn't known for his patience."

If *That* Gnome breaks a vase, the pieces will fall into patterns of great significance and meaning—but it is up to us to read and understand it. He is the potentially *constructive* force of chaos. *That* Gnome is also the keeper of our wild talents, the ones we may not even know we have. When he appears, it is often to call our attention to our latent gifts.

In a nutshell, which is where he claims to belong, his job is to help us get lost from our comfortable ruts so that we will explore wonderful, exciting, and strange new paths. He is a good friend of Raven, the philosopher-trickster, and Coyote is one of his many disguises. He is so smart that he sometimes outsmarts himself.

Can you laugh at yourself sometimes? And let the laughter carry you into new insights and new ways of being? Then *That* Gnome within you is waving his faery wand gleefully.

Starter Reading It's time to leap into the air, letting the earth turn beneath you, and discover where you come down again. Reasonable risks are okay. Even unreasonable risks are probably okay. Use your head and look before you leap, of course, but do so understanding that the actual jump is likely to be very rewarding. No guarantees, but then there never really are anyway, no matter how pretty the paper they may seem to be printed on and the scrollwork around the edge.

In a reading, the presence of *That* Gnome tells us that the forces of chaos are at work. Things may not be as they seem, and this may very well be a good thing. Look for the unexpected, find the opportunity in it, and go for it. He says that no matter how confused things may seem, there is a way to make them better—but it is a creative way, one you haven't tried before. He says, *"Think amazing new thoughts!"*

Reversed In a way, a trickster is always reversed, and sometimes even perverse. Sometimes, the reverse is even reversed into other dimensions. Standing on his head, *That* Gnome could be saying:

> *Be careful—there is trickery going on,* or
> *He who hesitates is lost,* or
> *Play it safe,* or
> *Fools rush in where angels fear to tread—but this isn't necessarily a bad thing because sometimes "fools" accomplish things that "angels" thought*

impossible, or

Complete honesty may not be the best policy, but lying is definitely *not the best policy,* or

Discretion is the better part of valor.

But which, you ask, is the *real* answer?

Oh, you want *that* kind of an answer? A neat one in a box? I'm sorry, but *That* Gnome doesn't do those kind of answers. He is just here to shake you up, jolt loose some preconceptions, help you to see yourself and your situation as it really is, and aid you in finding a new and unorthodox response. That's all.

Faery Guides and Guardians

The faery guides and guardians are those who devote time and energy to directly guiding humans as we develop our special talents and gifts and our own natural magic. They help us to become more than we already are, exploring our potentials and transcending our self-imposed limitations and fears. In some cases, they help us to climb out of the holes we have made for ourselves by misusing or misunderstanding our talents and potentials. They believe that a sense of humor is a necessary part of being a fulfilled and magical person, so they like to encourage this in us. Their jokes tend to be a bit more subtle than the Help-Line Troupe (starting on page 131), and that is probably just as well. A thing I've noticed, though, is that faeries in general don't think much of some of the human notions about "dignity" (read "pomposity"). They have a tendency to want to deflate whatever or whoever they see as overinflated. True dignity comes from being kind and showing respect and consideration for others and ourselves. It is not the slightest bit stuffy and is much admired by the faeries. You will find a lot of them have a great deal of it.

These faery guides also help us to discover the joys of living more harmoniously with nature, with each other, and with them. Every denizen of Faery is, in his or her or its own way, helping the worlds, ours and theirs, move toward greater harmony. We are, too, each in our own way.

Nelys the Alchemyst

Card 27—Nelys the Alchemyst

Inner transformation. Irrevocable change.

In Faery—and sometimes in our world—alchemy is the study and practice of transforming the soul from the lead of primitive conditioned reactions to the gold of spiritual and practical attainment. Nelys is mistress of the alchemical arts, and she also understands that daily life is a spiritual exercise. She recognizes that transformation may take place from the inside out or from the outside in. When things are stuck and movement has become impossible, Nelys firmly waves her rowan wand and things happen in ourselves and in the world.

Sometimes things just cannot move without readjustment—perhaps even radical realignment. We may feel that we *should* be able to bring our plans to fruition, but we may be aiming at the impossible, or at least at the very inappropriate. Part of the impossibility or inappropriateness may be a result of our own attitudes, beliefs, or behaviors, and part of it may be circumstances in the world—things that are beyond our control.

Often inner transformation is required in order to achieve what we wish for in the outer world, just as, conversely, changes in the outer world often elicit inner transformation. Personal inner change is the truest transformation of all—and in the long run, it is the only change that really matters.

"Nelys points out a path we can follow," Jonathan observes, "but she does not lead us by the hand along it—although she might give us a nudge, if we seem to need it."

When an Oracle group member was looking at Nelys, a giggling faery voice said, *"If you concentrate very hard, you can get to the* bottom *of the problem."*

Starter Reading When Nelys turns up in your reading, get ready for things to happen, inwardly and outwardly. The stuck becomes unstuck; the blocked begins to move. You may have to run to keep up with the speed at which the situation around you is moving. You may also be surprised by the direction things (and you) are taking. You may find your plans, even your desires and dreams, changing as the transformative process takes place. It might not have been in your plans, but later on you will look back and say, "Wow! It wasn't what I expected, but it was just what I needed."

When we have been through such an alchemical process, we can never go back to what we were before—which is probably just as well.

Reversed You may be getting in Nelys's way as she does her work. To put it bluntly, you may be the main obstacle in your own path. It may be necessary to transform attitudes and behaviors. She will first approach you with tact and a kindly faery warning, pointing out an alternate path you might try. At this point, it would be well to begin actively cooperating with her energy of alchemical transformation. That is quite a hefty faery wand she carries, and I'm sure it isn't just for decoration. I asked her about that, but I only got a outrageous grin in reply.

"Faeries hide what you want
and reveal what you need."
—*Brian*

Card 28—**Penelope Dreamweaver**
Inspiration. Magical dreams. Visions.

Weaver of dreams, bringer of visions, muse of artistic inspiration, Penelope weaves tapestries in the mind with threads of light, color, and sound. When she comes to us in dreams, we waken under her enchantment and rush for our paints or clay or other forms of expression.

28

Penelope Dreamweaver

In this painting, Brian has shown us Penelope, his own Inspiration Faery, but we each have an one who is more than willing to help us. Mine says to call her *Grace* because, she says, she isn't exactly someone I deserve—just someone I'm lucky enough to have in my life. She plays hard at inspiring me, as does Penelope with Brian. Penelope says she is *very* pleased with Brian's results of her inspirations, but when I looked hopefully at Grace to see what she thinks about me, she just shrugs her shoulders. Then she flashes me a wicked grin, so I *think* it is all right. Inspiration faeries like their jobs, but they get really bored when people don't *pay attention* to them. Then they sit around and file their fingernails while they think troublesome and mischievous thoughts. Sometimes they get exasperated enough to send us nightmares in an attempt to get us to *wake up!*

These faeries and their sisters, the Faeries of Expression, work together as teams, helping us in our creative endeavors. The Faeries of Inspiration sprinkle us with special inspirational faery dust so that we come up with ideas. *"Rather like fertilizing a plant, and you know what plants are fertilized with,"* Grace says. Then, their sisters, the Faeries of Expression, help us to give form to our creativity, manifesting it with our own particular talents.

Starter Reading Seek visions and inspiration. Be aware that they are often subtle and require close attention. Fantasies, dreams, and daydreams are all places an Inspiration Faery can contact us, but she can also pop up unannounced in the midst of the most ordinary of activities—in the bath, washing the dishes, driving the car, or anywhere else that our mind is half occupied and half running on idle. Pay special attention to unsought inspirations at this time. They have something wonderful to offer you, but it is up to you to catch them and bring them into reality.

Reverse You may feel that your creative expression is blocked or even dead. You may have been trying too hard, working too hard. This is a time to back off and do the things that renew and inspire you. Cut loose from the mundane world and give yourself time to enjoy your own fantasies and dreams. Then, choose what you want to bring into manifestation and begin to create it, even if you think you can't. Creation is one of the primary factors in the maintenance of sanity. Humor is another. So if you produce laughable results, you get two benefits for the one effort.

Alternatively, you may have been ignoring your Inspiration Faery's prompting, turning away from your own creativity. When we deny expression to our creative impulses, our creative energy tends to sour within us, causing problems with health, relationships, and other aspects of life. Denial of the possibilities put forth by our creative imaginations or allowing only the destructive possibilities of creativity to be considered are also serious problems, as is a refusal to learn from our dreams. Perhaps someone in this state of denial or blocking is also discouraging our creative impulses— or perhaps we are doing it to ourselves or others. If the first, the querent must learn to disregard this bad influence. If the second, an immediate change of attitude is urgently needed at this time.

Interestingly, Penelope and Grace tell me that whining about the "unfairness" of life instead of doing something to make it better is also linked with and a symptom of the suppression of one's creative energies.

Card 29 – Ta'Om the Poet
Clear sight. Poetry. Erotic energy. Laughter. Not getting into serious mischief.

For quite a while, as I looked at Ta'Om's portrait, I really didn't have a very clear idea of his character. He looks so serious, so pensive, so thoughtful— but that wasn't the energy I felt coming from him at all. He had me baffled and fooled. Then my son (also a member of the Oracle discussion group) looked at him and noted, "But he's wearing a mask—he's laughing at us. He likes to speed ahead of us, then stand inside a tree and watch us go by, thinking up mischief for us to fall into. Then he flows ahead, like a river, but

Ta'Om the Poet

much faster, up over the hills, and lies in wait for us."

That felt right, but Ta'Om looked at me with such wounded dignity that I almost got confused again. Then he started laughing and dashed off. I wondered some more about him, and one of the other faeries said, *"He's a fine traveling companion if you have a taste for adventure, bawdy songs, high flights of poetic fancy, and very, um, down-to-earth observations. A fine, fine fella!"*

Ta'Om's boundless curiosity leads him into some strange places, and he is quite happy to take us there with him. Ta'Om's wings, like ours, are neatly folded at his back and not readily visible. He is still learning to use them properly and thinks he is better with them than he really is. He wants to encourage us to unfold our wings and doesn't hesitate to lead us into situations where we almost have to fly (metaphorically, sometimes) in order to survive. When I was young, I think it was he who encouraged me to climb up lots of trees and high buildings I couldn't easily get down from, and I know it was he who encouraged my son to do similar things. He is very fond of children. Like him, they are usually willing to try anything.

Ta'Om has a poetic spirit, which involves much more than just the writing of rhymes. It is about being able to see things as they really are, and in that reality to recognize all beauty, even the beauty of necessity and difficulty. This is not an unthinking, reflexive, immature, "everything is for the best" attitude, but an understanding of the beauty of what we learn from joy and sorrow, from ease and hardship, from pain and pleasure. Ta'Om also wants to show us how silly it is to be so very solemn about life. He laughs at himself, he laughs at us—sometimes he laughs so hard he gets cowslip wine up his nose and then everyone else laughs at him. He doesn't mind that, as long as we are laughing.

Ta'Om is also the young apprentice shaman, barely beginning on the path but with a boundless interest in all things magical and mystical. He'll try anything and encourage you to do so as well, but you might find it advisable to show a little more sense than he does sometimes. He plays the panpipes, but not very well. He also chases the dryads and has much more success at this. He has a lust for life, wine, females, and song. He claims he was born on the Blarney Stone (which I doubt) and consequently has a wonderful gift for words (which I don't doubt at all). He loves children, writers, and blithe, adventurous, uninhibited spirits. He is a storyteller with a great imagination and has the power to inspire others to action with his words.

Starter Reading When Ta'Om turns up in a reading, his presence suggests that youthful spirits and energy abound. This is the time to do exciting things and to tackle projects you've been wanting to do but for which you perhaps felt you didn't have the time or energy. It may even be the time to write about them, but you probably need to *do* them first.

Ta'Om often shows up in readings for people who have a talent and inclination for writing—poetry, adventure, fantasy, or anything else. Possibly the only thing he ever gets very serious about is his writing, and he will spend all the time he needs searching for *just* the right word. Speaking and writing with conviction and sincerity and the ability to persuade others are indicated by Ta'Om's presence, along with an outpouring of ideas.

You may also find yourself thinking about romance and deciding that you want more of it in your life. This doesn't necessarily mean looking for someone new; it might well involve putting some romantic fizz into a relationship that has become overly routine.

Reversed This card reversed can indicate confusion about what is really true, or it may suggest that we are being silent when in fact we need to speak up. It can also indicate lies found out. You can get into a lot of trouble with Ta'Om. Just use a little common sense. If you don't have much, here is your chance to develop some instead of spending your brain energy making up excuses for foolishness. This card reversed in a reading suggests that exercising good sense is of some urgency lest you wind up head over heels like the reversed Ta'Om.

The Laume

Card 30—The Laume

Unconditional giving. Unconditional receiving.

She is *the* Laume in the same way that *the* Macgregor is the chief of the Clan Macgregor—*the* Laume of all Laumes. *The* Laume is a charitable soul in the old sense of the word charity, which is loving and giving. She knows the joy of giving without expectation of return. From practicing this ourselves, we learn that there always *is* a return, often from the least expected source. The universe likes to keep its accounts up to date, and *the* Laume's job is to encourage us to keep the credit side of our cosmic accounts balanced by freely giving. We have been given the earth, the sun, the stars, and the moon. We have been given trees and flowers and things to eat and a multitude of prospective friends. It's going to take a considerable amount of generosity to come into balance with all those gifts we have already received.

When we fall out of balance in what we give and what we receive, we can have constipation or diarrhea of the spirit. Spiritual constipation makes us toxic and bloated and unable to deal with more intake. Spiritual diarrhea makes us energetically depleted, limp, and needy. The spiritual forms of these particular malfunctions are entirely a result of our choices about balancing our giving and receiving. You may think you have it right, but if things are not going well for you, *the* Laume suggests you think again.

If you are pushing and pushing at something, it can often help greatly just to back off, relax about it, and let the energy flow. If at the same time that you back up from your efforts, you put energy into the universe elsewhere, then energy just naturally has to flow back to you in the most appropriate and generous form. The universe also has to keep its accounts balanced.

Studying *the* Laume's picture, a discussion group member wrote,

"*The* Laume is still bugging me. She looks passive, but watchful. I think she feels that this giving business needs a bit more explanation. It is about being ready to do that sometimes quite small thing just when it is needed. A pinch of fairy dust in just the right place at just the right time works wonders—but big clouds of fairy dust just makes everyone sneeze."

This is true. Sometimes a small bit of helpfulness now prevents a big need later. And sometimes a big thing is needed right from the beginning.

Another Oracle reader noted that *the* Laume's wings looked a bit tattered and wondered if this indicated that it is sometimes appropriate to give until it hurts. "*Yes, it is,*" *the* Laume says. "*Not as a habit, not as a sort of martyrdom, but only on the rare occasions when it is truly needed.*"

One of *the* Laume's charming customs is to give through whatever pair of hands is nearest—providing they allow her to do so. Do you let *the* Laume give through your hands or do you put them in your pockets and hold back, holding on to what is "yours"? If so, you are missing a lot of fun, some interesting experiences—and spiritual growth.

Starter Reading If you are stuck or blocked in a situation and *the* Laume turns up in a reading, you probably need to stop focusing on what you are trying to accomplish and simply give to others—freely and generously and unconditionally.

Try a few random acts of kindness, unconditionally given, of course. Go do some volunteer work somewhere. Mow your elderly neighbor's lawn or take homemade soup or some flowers from your garden to someone you know who is ill. Give some help to a coworker just because they need it. Give to a needy stranger, whether or not you think he deserves it. Take flowers into a hospital and give them to a stranger at random. Or give them to a nurse, with compliments from the universe. Give a bit more than you think you can afford; go a little further than you think you reasonably can. Empty your wallet or purse of all your cash for a beggar on the street. Don't worry—it will fill up again, much faster than you might expect.

Reverse Ask yourself if you have been giving too much and it is time to stop and attend to your own needs for a bit. Alternatively, ask yourself if you have been refusing to receive the bounty of the universe flowing through *the* Laume's hands, just because it wasn't in quite the form that you expected or because it was from a different source than you wanted it to

UnDressing of a Salad

come from. Sometimes we put restrictions on our receiving. For example, we may feel that approval and love has to come from one specific person or all other approval and love is without value to us. If so, we need to learn to accept what comes from any source as coming from a loving universe, blessed by _the_ Laume's hands.

Card 31—UnDressing of a Salad

Balance. Avoiding extremes.
Achieving the impossible.
Being impossible.

Brian called this painting _The Dressing of a Salad_, but in an earlier stage of the _Good Faeries / Bad Faeries_ manuscript it was _The Undressing of a Salad_. I've combined the names because they show us important aspects of the card. The dressing of a salad requires a good balance—disparate elements must blended into a tasty whole. The _un_dressing of a salad requires truly remarkable adroitness. At first, one might think it impossible, but Adroito, whom we see busily balancing magical balls, is the Faery of Doing Impossible Things. He is also the Faery of Being Impossible and the Faery of Avoiding Extremes. Sound impossible? Well, _of course_ it is.

Both Adroito and Sally (crouched above him) are intently focused on balancing things, and the large gnome in the center finds this very amusing. He looks in two directions at once, seeing the impossibility of _keeping_ things that are in constant motion in balance at all times—like the juggling act of life. Of _course_ we fall out of balance. Of _course_ we occasionally drop the ball. Sometimes we drop the ball (or a bird flies by and snatches it from us) and we just have to invent another one. Sometimes this seems as impossible as undressing a salad.

There are times when we have to turn bad luck into good —and that isn't always easy, especially if someone else seems determined to turn good luck into bad. Everything is integrating and disintegrating at the same time. Confusion is rife, but we still try to create order and put things into balance. The whole universe is hurtling through time at an astonishing rate, and it is very difficult to keep balance on a rapidly moving object, especially as it appears to lurch unpredictably from time to time. Sooner or later Adroito or Sally (or both) will drop their balls. The sulky-looking fellow on the left is clearly waiting to snatch one or two so that he can play, too—or maybe just so that Adroito and Sally cannot. My money is on Adroito, though. He is smart enough to realize that old balls wear out and new ones must be brought into play. He is ready to deal with this. The balance changes constantly, but it is still balance.

Starter Reading Things are in motion and the outcome is impossible to predict. A cool head is required to deal with this, as is a readiness to jump in whatever direction seems appropriate. Exercise cool judgment while staying ready for the unpredictable. Sudden changes of fortune may appear good or bad, but they are in flux and can be rechanneled if necessary. Develop poise, stay calm. You can come out a winner here, but it is likely to take concentrated effort. Use power with delicacy and discretion.

Reversed Imbalance occurs. Confusion happens. Lovely balls fall on the floor, and we discover that they are uncooked eggs. Sleight of hand may be happening and things that appear to be so are not—and vice versa. Misdirection may be prevalent. Attempts at overcontrol may be contributing to the problem. Someone may be attempting unethical or unkind manipulations.

However, it is worth remembering that out of chaos we can sometimes create miracles. After all, Unity (Card 1) created the whole universe that way.

Card 32 – Iris of the Rainbows
Hope. Promise for the future.

Blue skies and rain are the realm of Iris, the Rainbow Faery. She dwells at the meeting of air (the element of mind) and water (the element of emotion). She sits, rainbow-hued wings outspread, suspended in midair, partially wrapped in her deep-sky draperies and crowned with iris blossoms. The faery archers tip their arrows in her potent handful of iridescent light.

Iris of the Rainbows

Firing their arrows, they send poly-chromatic rays into the storm, bringing light to dismal skies and hope to darkened hearts.

Beneath the Rainbow Faery, the amphibious creatures of a wet earth crouch. The faery frog maiden and the frog (anyone care to kiss him and see what happens?) peer out from their shelter at the storm-wracked world, while the shadowed sun is dimly seen above Iris's head. Sturdy, potbellied gnomes, their toes rooted in the earth, sport sweeping whiskers to prove their entitlement to their single iris crowns, while the helpful faery amphibians hold transparent, rainbow-filled globes for the Rainbow Faery. Everyone, especially Iris herself, is fully absorbed in the task of reclaiming the bright sky from the dark of the storm.

In her hand, the light of heaven's bow looks a fragile thing, yet it is the light of hope, the promise of healing and joy to come, and that is one of the most powerful things there is.

Starter Reading Iris tells us that light is breaking through our present darkness, and that hope is a powerful factor in speeding up this process. She does not promise us that the storm is over, nor does she say that it will never storm again, but she does say that there is brightness and beauty here. She also tells us that there is something to be gained by this passage through the storm. And the sooner we learn what it is, the sooner the storm will end.

Always, a passage through the storm is a time of potential growth, a time to allow the dead wood of our past to be blown away to make room for the green shoots of new growth. At this point, it is useful to ask ourselves what we still need to release, and to look after protecting and nurturing the seeds we have planted. Iris suggests that the cultivation of patience may also be helpful at this time.

The storm is breaking up. Are we ready for the change? If we are presently frogs, the faeries say, the time of our transformation, foretold by the rainbow, may be at hand. Then we shall be kissed by the puissant light of the sun—and discover if we are still frogs or if we have become something much more.

Reversed It is true that there is hope and there is promise for the future, but it is at present obscured or delayed. There may well be more trials to be met before we come to the end of this storm. Iris reminds us that hope, prayer, and faith may be needed, that help is there if we ask for it, though it may not come in the form we request. She reminds us, in these difficult times, to remember our aspirations, to consider who it is that we are trying to become, and to hold those images surrounded by her prismatic light in our minds as we pass through this time of darkness. All times of hardship offer us the same challenge: to grow or to diminish. The choice is ours, but she is ready to lighten our path if we will accept her offering into our hearts. No storm, no darkness, lasts forever.

"Winged female faeries are the soul's messengers, representing the spirit freed from the mundane. They are creatures of aspiration and transcendence, flying between the worlds, between heaven and earth, between the body and the soul."
—Brian

Card 33—Faeries of the Future
Be here NOW. Guidance. Moving forward.

The Gnome of Now at the top of the card looks both ways simultaneously, something that would give a human a crick in the brain if he tried it. However, the gnome has no particular problem with this, as faeries always have a sliding sense of past, present, and future. Anna, in the center, steps boldly forth, pregnant with possibilities and carrying the hazelnut that grants wisdom. Puggi, above her, crouches ready to take off and rush ahead just as

Faeries of the Future

soon as she is sure what direction they are going, while the frog above her waits, hoping to be kissed, just to see what will happen. Amalatheia, on the left, hesitates momentarily, not sure she is dressed properly or has her hair done right for the occasion. Nearly everyone looks to the future with cheerful optimism.

For all of Anna's bold stepping forward, if you look closely you can see that she has her eyes on the wise Gnome King at the lower left. *He* seems sure of the way to go. He is relying on his gut sense to guide him, knowing that this is his magic and it will serve him better than logic in the unknown future. Being a gnome, a son of earth, he is well grounded in reality, which is what it takes to have trustworthy gut feelings. Anna, being wise, or at least very nearly so, trusts him in this. Of course, she hasn't considered that where he wants to go may not be where she would most like to be. Fortunately, he *has* considered that and is pointing her in the right direction.

The pleasingly plump gnome lady admiring the Gnome King from her mushroom hopes to be invited on the journey, though she would do better to invite herself, like all the others, instead of waiting. The old Oak Man in the lower right is firmly rooted in the present and has no desire to travel in space. His journey is through time only, as he contemplates the wisdom of stillness and deep roots. He is contented, serene, and wise because this life suits him, and he has learned to make the best of what he has. He is happy to watch the other faeries pass by. It suits him, but this is not a way most faeries and humans usually choose to live.

Both humans and faeries are constantly adventuring into the future, being carried there by Old Father Time and Earthmother, acting hand in hand. Even the galaxies spin into the future, creating strange effects and relationships between time and space and light. He who hesitates doesn't get lost—he gets dragged along, will he, nill he, bumping bruisingly behind the rest. He might as well get up and hustle along too—it's ever so much nicer a way to travel.

These faeries are on an exciting journey to co-create the future with the universe, just as we are. They greet each rising dawn and each rising moon with unconditional and expectant gratitude. Join them.

Starter Reading Brian writes, "These are the faeries of a bright future and are essential companions on any journey. When these faeries appear, it is time to consider where we have been and where we wish to go." There are many opportunities, many potentials, but we must choose a path and then take realistic, practical steps to bring the desired future into being. This is not a time to wait for things to come to us, but to step forward boldly to meet them. We may do this alone, if we wish, or in the company of those who share our goals and dreams.

Reversed Are you certain you are going in the direction that *you* wish to go—or are you merely following someone else's lead without being clear about your own direction? It may be that you need to consider a parting of the ways if the goals of others do not match yours or if they seem to be headed in a direction that is not right for you. This is the moment to pause and consider your direction. Think where you would like to be and *who* you would like to be a quarter of a century from now. Ask yourself if the steps you are considering now are apt to take you closer to that goal or farther from it. Ask the wise Gnome King to point a clear direction for you.

Card 34—Sylvanius
Truth. Cutting through deception. Clarity.

Brian called this painting *The Mask of Truth, True Dreaming.* Sylvanius, who holds the Mask of Truth, is lord of the woodlands, his crown of antler branches signifying his authority. He presents the mask to us, supported by the Faery of Aspiration, as she welcomes us to our own potential. We wear the mask to look inward, seeing our true selves—not our false and fearful selves, but the beings of light that we truly are and what we have the potential to be. It becomes very difficult for us to make excuses and blame others for our failures and fears once we have seen what we *could* be if we were willing—what, in fact, we already are but are not quite living up to.

I thought it was very odd that there is a Mask of Truth. It seemed to

Sylvanius

me that we use masks to *hide* truth rather than to reveal it.

"*Oh, no!*" Sylvanius assured me. "*First, you put the mask on and hide, and then you take it off to reveal the truth.*" Very faery.

"I see," I said, not certain I did, but not sure I wanted to either.

"*Besides,*" Sylvanius continued, "*your face is not your Truth. Sometimes faces need to be hidden so Truth can be seen. Or sometimes you need to make a crack in consciousness—an aha! moment—in order to see a truth you have been blind to.*"

From before the time we were born, people have been projecting their ideas, hopes, fears, and confusions on us. As we grow up, we accept many of these untrue projections as our reality—our partly false, partly true picture of ourselves.

Brian wrote, "The faery, Kundrun, holds one of the many sacred swords of Faeryland. This one, forged long ago by mysterious dwarves, is laid across the cliff of the otherworld as a bridge to Faeryland. The two-edged sword symbolizes the union of the human world with the world of Faery, as well as the union of the outer world of nature with the inner world of the psyche. It is the sword of clear-cut understanding and sharp perception. But once we cross into Faery it becomes the sword of courage and noble service."

Starter Reading At this time you are discovering new truths about yourself. They are essential for you to know in order to create relationships based on mutual respect, affection, and trust. These things can only work if we see ourselves and others as we are. Currently, both Faery and this world are functioning as a giant mirror in which we see ourselves in many surprising ways. People tend to dread this because we assume that we are worse than we think we are, but this is far from necessarily true. Now is a time for finding out the false and misleading beliefs you have accepted and discovering that you are a better person than you thought—and have the potential to accomplish more than you believed you could. If someone says you are better or simply different than you think you are, don't automatically reject this. Think it over carefully. You have more to give and more to enjoy than you have been giving yourself credit for.

Reverse Sylvanius, Kundrun, and the Faery of Aspiration have ganged up on you. They are creating cracks in your ideas about yourself so that the light of truth may shine in. Mirrors jump out at us with unexpected reflections. The trick is learning to distinguish the distorted reflections of others' masks of untruth from the clear reflection of the Mask of Truth. Beware of the reflections that others cast upon you and look within for your own truth. Whenever someone says, "Oh, you are so . . . ," stop and ask yourself if this is really true. It might just be their stuff, their projections, and have nothing to do with you at all.

Card 35 – The Faun
Understanding the nature of Nature. Natural wisdom. Natural magic.

The merry, irrepressible Faun, dancing in the garden, frolicking in the woods, playing in the meadows, sings out, *"Come, dance with me!"* It is he who knows the secrets of nature. He knows where the robin's nestlings are hidden, where the mice lurk, who lives down that rabbit burrow, and where the pixies like to dance.

He teaches us to understand, appreciate, and express the part of ourselves that dances in the moonlight with the faeries, sings to the dawn stars with the birds, and hums with the blossoming flowers. This is also the part of us that plants seeds with a loving pat that says, "Bless you and grow," and provides healing energy (see "Faery-Style Readings") for doing just that. No fuss, no bother, just intention and natural human magic.

Natural magic is simple. We are all full of it—and the more we are true to our own nature, the more we have access to our own magic. When we are caught up in believing in limitations imposed by ourselves or our culture, we inhibit the flow of energy, which is the melody of Ekstasis's song of the cosmos (Card 2) as it sweeps through us. Opening ourselves back up to that song can be a long and complex business once we have closed down in

The Faun

some way. It requires a great deal of thought and self-observation, and perhaps also the help of others in the form of formal therapy or simple friendship. However, the process of opening is made easier and more gentle if we allow Mama Nature and our own natural magic to help.

Spending time in our gardens, our parks, our forests, and open spaces helps us to reconnect, but so does growing herbs and flowers and scented geraniums in pots on our windowsills. So does looking at the stars, observing the state of the sky, and listening to the wind. It helps if we simply observe the natural processes and changes around us.

Mama Nature is always up to something; no natural place is the same for two moments in a row. Life is about process, not stasis. *We* are processes, not things. We constantly change, even when we resist, even when we think we are stuck. *"Come with me!"* sings the Faun, tugging our hand. It certainly is futile to struggle against the flow of the universe, so we might as well dance with him. Stuckness is an illusion. The Faun says, *"Dance with me, and it will all come right!"* And, do you know? He's right. At least, many of the blocks in ourselves and our lives will come right much more quickly if we reconnect with him, opening our hearts to him and Mama Nature. They, too, are filled with magic. Just like us.

Starter Reading Natural magic is happening. When things flow almost effortlessly, that is a sign that natural magic is at work. Enjoy it! A very important part of natural magic is simply allowing the energy to flow through us. This means both giving and receiving freely. Let the energy flow—don't push it, don't try to control it; just dance with it. Trust it. And remember to keep returning to the source for inspiration and to keep your heart filled with light.

Reverse This situation—and probably the people involved—have become bogged down in murky energy and need a breath of wild, fresh air blown through them. Organize a picnic or go for walks in the park or the country with any others involved, and invite the faeries to come along and help you harmonize the atmosphere. If you can't do that, give the other people a gift of potted plants, preferably with flowers. Come back to your natural self. Be aware of the cycles of sun and moon, the ever changing, flowing balance of Mama Nature. Live in harmony with that. Exercise appropriately. Eat well. Clear the toxins of "civilized" living from your system. Go out and speak to Lady Moon as often as you can. Smile back at Father Sun.

Card 36—Spirit Dancer
Self-expression. Freedom. Exploration.

The Spirit Dancer understands both sides of self-expression. In the first stage we get our inner vision, feelings, and creative impulse out into the world through our art, whatever that is. Then our expressions are reflected back to us from the mirror of other people's perceptions, and we discover what our art awakens in them.

First and most important for many of us, we learn, grow, and lead more satisfying lives if we have ways of expressing our inner world. Such expressions can be a way of helping ourselves better understand our feelings and experiences. Or they can be a way of getting pain out where we can look at it and let it begin to heal. Creative expression is a method of exploring our own truth, bringing it into the light so we can see it more clearly, and maintaining sanity. The key words here are *explore, experiment*, and *express*. As this faery cryptically remarked to one Oracle reader, *"The Death of Spirit Dancer is Perfection."*

Second, creative expression is a way of sharing and letting others see more of our true selves. It is a way that we can reach out from this illusion of separation and reaffirm our essential connections with one another. When we share a dance, a painting, or a poem with others, we do so with the hope that they will see something of what we have put into it and that their experience will echo ours in some way. But if we have done well, we will be able to add something to their experience. At the same time, we understand that their slant on things is a bit different and that what they reflect back to us by their response will perhaps contain something we haven't seen about our own experience—a new insight, a different view, an expansion of our picture of reality. So this side of creative expression, the sharing part, enriches us in a different way than the actual creation. I have never written a poem or sculpted something without the experience changing me—and then changing me again when I shared it with others. This is something I've heard many others say, including many who do not consider themselves "real artists" or "real writers."

Spirit Dancer encourages us to take creative action from our place of personal power, the inner core of true feelings and understanding within us. She wants us to clarify our vision, find the creative potential that lies hidden in paradox, confusion, and chaos, and turn these into a free-flowing, finely balanced, evolving order. She wants to aid us in making our best fantasies real.

She also is very enthusiastic about helping us to learn to dance well with the faeries, if we don't already know how. And if we do know how, she would still be delighted to dance with us just for the fun of it. Step out boldly!

Starter Reading Now is the time to focus and really concentrate on a project or process, especially one involving the creative arts. Spontaneity balanced by self-discipline will help us achieve our goals. Strive for elegance and simplicity. This is a time to bring out and share qualities that we have nurtured in private.

Reverse Self-absorbed and obsessed, the reversed Spirit Dancer has become entangled in her own unexpressed and perhaps inexpressible fantasies. She feels angry and driven, and may be unable to express her feelings in any way except through destruction.

Alternatively, this card may speak of the artist's block. The cure for that is to just create. Even if the creation falls far short of our goals, even if it is trite or trivial, *just do it*. It is a matter of priming the pump until the waters of creativity, emotion, and inspiration flow freely.

Card 37 — Tobaira of the Waters

Emotions. Serenity. Meditation. Gracefully accepting change.

For a moment, close your eyes and just let yourself feel the cool, sparkling faery waters flowing through your fingers. Imagine drinking this sparkling coolness from your own cupped hands, and imagine the water flowing down your throat. You may even be able to feel that magical, energy-filled coolness flow right through you to your toes.

Ah! Feel better?

Throughout the world, there are healing wells, both for general health and specific ailments. In modern times, many of their faery qualities have been diluted, even though Tobaira and her healing helpers do all that they can to keep them clear and potent. Faery waters reflect the emotional state of the human people around them, so the faery waters that come through to our world have lessened in purity and power in places where people are living especially stressful "civilized" lives. As one Oracle group member observes, "There are profound connections with drinking water, tears, wells of forgiveness, water as the fluid of transforming nutrients in the body, the connecting flow . . . I could flow on and on but I'll stop."

However, the many healing faeries who help Tobaira do the best they can under the circumstances to purify the waters, and they try to maintain their own merry spirits to give added power to the waters. We can help the faeries by creating more merriment in the lives of others and in our own lives.

In addition to the healing wells, there are wells and springs that bestow wisdom or skill upon the drinker, like the famous Hippocrene fountain on Mount Helicon, which bestows poetic inspiration. I suspect it of being a faery fountain because of the way it works. If you have one drink, you gain a certain level of poetic ability, another draught brings you more, and the third brings you to the full flower of poetry. The reason the world is not overrun with magnificent poets is because, first, it is very difficult to find the spring, and second, the water packs such a wallop that most people stagger off after a single drink or two. And you only get one chance at the spring. There are also the fountains of youth, like the one on Dun I, the highest hill on Iona, a magical isle on the west coast of Scotland. I looked and looked for this fountain, but didn't find it. I shall have to try again next time I'm there, because I am much more in need of it now than I was all those years ago.

Starter Reading Water is mutable, changeable, fluid, and Tobaira speaks to us of a particular kind of change—change of emotions and possibly a change in health. We have important choices to make about how we meet those changes and where we let them take us—toward the calm, flowing purity of the faery waters or the boiling cauldron of hot temper and steamy emotions. The choice is obvious, but we sometimes forget that we have it. Tobaira reminds us that we do have a choice—and making it, wisely or unwisely, determines our future.

The things we need in life remain constant, no matter what is going on or how hectic the changes and pressures in our life may be. We need nurturing and love, and it is ultimately up to us to provide that for ourselves. The healing faeries will help us if we ask them to.

Reverse This can indicate emotional needs not met, or thirst of the spirit or emotions. Or, on the other hand, it can remind us that faery spells on waters can be mischievous, causing confusion, muddled memory, and irritability in humans. Perhaps a cold shower is in order here. Certainly, it is a time for cooling off, calming down, and quieting the waters of our emotions before we take any action.

Card 38—Laiste, Moon's Daughter

Light cast in shadows. Spiritual guidance. Illumination. Riddles.

Laiste, Moon's Daughter

She is the bringer of light in the darkness, yet moonlight both reveals and conceals. Her bright faery hoofprints light the path ahead of you, guiding you through the dark. She is also one of the guides at the passages between the otherworlds and this one. It is she who, with her bright light, tends the Gate of Revelation, showing us the way through by illumination, while her sister, Epona's Wild Daughter (Card 54) helps guide us through the Gate of Despair. Laiste's gate is much more fun.

Yet, in the process of guiding us, Laiste may pull a veil of cloud across the face of her mother, the moon—and three steps later we fall into a bog. "That *should wake you up*," she thinks, smiling wisely. She disapproves of sleepwalking, which is something that most of us humans do a great deal of the time. The night contains too much magic and beauty and wisdom to walk through it unseeing. You may find her activities helpful; you may find them frustrating. How you take them is entirely up to you, but they are intended to help you awaken. Bear in mind that she does not trip us; she merely places an obstacle or a pitfall in our path, and we, sleepwalking and unaware, step right into it. We don't have to do that. As always, it is our choice.

Laiste wants us to be open to the great unknown, to mystical (not necessarily magical) experiences that teach us an expanded way to relate to the multiverse, all of the worlds and dimensions together. She is daughter of the moon, but she is also an illumined child of Unity (Card 1). Where the Losgunna, the Frog Queen (Card 39), wishes you to get in touch with your subconscious and find the treasures there, Laiste hopes you will reach for your higher self, your not-yet-realized cosmic wisdom. You know far more than you know you know.

There are places in ourselves that we may have feared because they are shadowed and unknown. We may imagine them full of monsters when, in fact, they are inhabited by joyful spirits. She wishes us to explore this terra incognita because that is where much of our potential and as yet unexplored wisdom lies. Laiste reaches into our deepest minds, opening long-shut doors, illuminating and revealing the uncultivated ground of our being—our hidden senses and talents. She speaks to us in the language of symbols, as faeries often do, because words are so limited. Any one symbol may speak to us on many levels of consciousness and about many different aspects of being, if we spend time contemplating it. Laiste is a sphinx, and finding the answers to her profound riddles gives us keys to the multi-verse.

If you are attending to your dreams and visions and studying every-day occurrences, trying to discover the deeper levels of meaning in the symbols there, you are learning the language of Laiste. That language is spoken by artists, like Brian, and poets, whose works are informed by rich symbolism. Discovering it through study, through looking within ourselves, and through interaction with faeries not only teaches us the language of Faery, of art, and of high poetry, but it also gives us keys to our own psychic abilities and to the deep levels of our own psyches, where the Singers and the creative force of Unity are most easily found.

Through revelation and the ecstatic experience of the mystic, Laiste faces and leads us into the future. She prefers to let the old stuff of the past fade away in the illumination of insight and newly accessed wisdom.

Starter Reading You may be finding apparently random events and ideas are falling into a pattern and beginning to make sense to you. Things may be flowing more easily than you are accustomed to, and your decisions and choices may be bringing an unusually high degree of success. Psychic abili-ties—hunches, intuitions, foreknowings—are becoming clearer and making more sense. Trust the process.

Laiste also brings psychic dreams, forelighting the future and illu-mining the present. These dreams often speak in symbols, as faeries are wont to do.

Reverse If someone is experiencing free-floating anxiety, inexplicable self-doubt, or a tendency to accidents, it may be that change is occurring at the very deep levels of the psyche. In various stages of such work, as change takes place on a deeply unconscious level, some disruptive energies rise to the surface of consciousness. Be especially careful and watchful as you go through your daily activities. When we are occupied on these deep levels with change, many of our automatic coping mechanisms fail to work properly. We are too busy deeper down to pay attention to whether or not the traffic light is red or the shoe laces are untied.

Alternatively, this card reversed may indicate that Laiste is working behind the scenes with others to bring about change—which, in turn, will probably eventually elicit change in the querent.

This card reversed can also signify that someone is unreasonably and unrealistically demanding superhuman perfection from others. Laiste's advice on this is, *"Don't!"*

Another alternative is that by ignoring dreams, portents, omens, and insights that are trying to occur at this deep level, someone is denying or blocking change. Laiste does what she can, but when her help is refused, she refers people to her sister, Dorcha, Epona's Wild Daughter (Card 54).

Card 39 —Losgunna
Sunken treasure. Discovery of self. Adventure.

The realm of Losgunna, the Frog Queen, is extensive, both below and above the waters. Faery waters are made up of human emotions, sometimes beautifully clear and sparkling and sometimes disgustingly murky. Different faeries are attracted to different waters. You would hardly expect to find the Soul Shrinker (Card 55) or old Gloominous Doom (Card 56) happily splashing in clear or sparkling waters, although you might find Nelys the Alchemyst (Card 27) at a murky pool, holding her nose as she waves a clarifying wand over it. Most of the bright faeries avoid such places. However, Losgunna knows that there are treasures, lost in disasters or abandoned by pirates, to be found in the murkiest of waters.

Exploration is what this card is all about, and through exploring and seeing what we really are, warts and all (Losgunna would like you to know that *she* doesn't have warts), we discover parts of our talents and potentials that have been hidden by old traumas and misunderstandings, or by

Losgunna

lack of opportunity. Losgunna's explorations are not limited to the realm of the emotions but also include the world. She wants us to dive deeply into new experiences—even if the new experiences involve flying high. Listen to different styles of music with open ears, try new tastes, look at new sights, and try them all with the open willingness of a child. She especially wants us to explore new ideas.

Have you ever noticed how people tend not to explore the territory they live in? How they only visit the special places there when they are trying to entertain someone from out of town? We do the same thing with so many aspects of our lives, and then, sometimes, we grumble that life is dull. Life is *always* adventurous for adventurous people and boring for boring people. My grandmother told me this when I was nine, and I expect she got it from Losgunna. She also told me that if I didn't have anything interesting to do, I might as well clean up my room. I took this lesson to heart and so can you. If life seems boring and you feel stuck in your puddle, either explore the parts of the puddle you haven't really seen before or jump out and do something new and interesting. I'm sure you, dear reader, are not a bored or boring person—boring people don't read books like this.

Starter Reading Losgunna tells us to pay attention to our dreams, to listen to the murmur of the waters, to note the patterns in the damp, fallen leaves, to listen for the distant, high sounds of angelic music among the stars. She also suggests soothing baths, hot tubs, Jacuzzis, trips to the nearest spa or hot springs, and dips in the handiest sea, pond, or mountain lake. Mud baths also help us quiet down and become strong enough to explore her territory, which is the earth and the waters, from the depths to the heights.

As important as it is to explore the inner realms, she tells us that exploration of the outer realms is also vital. She suggests that we go places we have never been, try things we have never done, take classes in subjects we always meant to study someday, maybe even learn a language and see where that takes us. Explore widely and deeply in our own world so that we develop the adventurousness of our spirits.

It almost goes without saying that she recommends exploring Faery. She also suggests kissing any metaphorical or actual frogs you encounter to test for princes or princesses—but I don't know how seriously you want to take that suggestion.

Reverse Bored? Tired of the same old same thing? A question we must ask ourselves is are we boring as well as bored? The message here is to try the things suggested above (or invent our own) before Gawtcha (Card 64) takes pity on us and liberates us from our firmly stuck-in-the-mud state. It is *so* much more fun to jump than to be pushed.

The Help-Line Troupe

These are the "wee folk" of Faery, large and small, who sometimes assist us in our daily lives—and sometimes add more than a little to the confusion, usually in an effort to be helpful. These faeries are associated with the five elements: earth, air, fire, water, and moonlight. Some of them work singly and some are trouping faeries. All are full of life and fun and generally sassy and often mischievous. They are the ones we often think of when we think of brownies and pixies and such. *"Except,"* Faery Nuff says, *"when we are thinking of another sort of faery altogether."*

They asked me to remind you here that, while they are willing to meet you anywhere, they particularly like to play with you out in the natural world, practicing natural magic. I said I thought that was very sensible, and Faery Nuff, often a spokesfaery, replied, *"Yes, but that's no reason to not do it."*

He now adds, apropros of nothing I can see, *"What a man sows, that shall he reap, as the silly man said as he sowed the meal."*

As Brian wrote, "Faeries are irrational, poetic, absurd, and very, very wise."

Honesty

Card 40 —Honesty

Honesty. Compassion. Tact.
Self-deceit.

Just look at him! Could you doubt for a moment that he sees you just as you are? And loves you anyway?

In plant form, which is how we may see him most often, Honesty makes lovely purple flowers in the spring and later on produces those silvery-white circular seed pods, like small images of the full moon. These little earth-moon seed pods remind us to reflect upon our reactions and feelings, to throw light into our darknesses, and to deal honestly with ourselves and others.

Honesty's other botanical names are Moonwort, Satin Flower, Silver Dollar, Moneywort, Dollar Plant, Penny Flower, Bolbonac, and, on Monday, the moon's day, he is Lunaria annua. Honesty is said to repel monsters. I don't have any monsters handy to check this out on, but I can certainly see the metaphorical truth in it. He is also known as Unshoe-the-Horse because of his habit of unshoeing horses who tread upon him—a very faery thing to do, and who can blame him? He is said to have collected thirty horseshoes from the horses of the Earl of Essex on the White Downs in Devonshire, near Tiverton. Let that be a lesson to you not to tread Honesty underfoot.

Starter Reading Honesty in a reading speaks, unsurprisingly, of the need for straight dealing and truth in representation. We need to be scrupulously honest here, making certain that there is no room for confusion or misunderstanding, no fuzzy edges. Both written and verbal agreements need to be completely clear. Assumptions may not be as well understood by all parties as we are assuming and they need to be tested for comprehension.

On a personal level, Honesty reminds us not only to be clear in what we say and do, but also to act and speak with compassion and tact. Brutal honesty is not usually true honesty at all, but somehow slanted toward the worst. Dishonesty, even in the name of tact, is not helpful either. Balancing on that fine line of loving honesty may take some effort, but will provide rich rewards. Honest humility, idealism, and clarity of mind are some of the advantages of honesty.

Reverse Honesty asks us, are we being truly honest with *ourselves*? We may think we are, but finding Honesty standing on his head in a reading indicates that we may well be deceiving ourselves in some way. The human psychological mechanisms (repression, denial, projection, displacement, et cetera) may be in play. We need to look carefully at our attitudes and beliefs, especially where our emotions are strongly involved. We may even need objective, clear-sighted assistance from others in looking at this. Self-deceit leads to anxiety, confusion, a complicated life, and behaving with unfairness or injustice toward oneself and others.

Card 41 —Ilbe the Retriever
Office of Unclaimed Property, Hopes, and Wishes. Loyalty.

While writing this, I was having a little trouble with Ilbe—not for the first time. I couldn't find my keys anywhere. He thinks it would be greatly to my benefit to be more organized and tidy, so he smears not-quite-visible juice on things that are out of place. Or he encourages the resident cats to hide things. (Cats seem remarkably willing to cooperate with these little bits of faery helpfulness.) Then I have to hunt and hunt for them, and Ilbe hopes I shall be more organized the next time. You may have encountered him in this guise. When he has done something like this, my son observes, he just looks at us with that "Who? Me?" look. My son also advises, "Keep your eye on him and whatever isn't nailed down. And if you scold or contradict him, he just gets huffy and insists on having his own way."

    This sort of busybody helpfulness is just one of Ilbe's tasks, however. He also has more important things to do.

    Ilbe is a protector. He retrieves and safeguards our lost hopes, forgotten dreams, and mislaid keys. (My keys were under a stack of papers, stuck to the floor with peach juice—not a place that I'd put them myself, but certainly safe from most key thieves.) He holds these seeds of our potential futures carefully and delicately until we are ready for their return.

41

Ilbe ~ the Retriever

Sometimes we don't think we are ready for them or we have given up hope altogether, and then he may arrange reminders for us—events or people in our lives that bring back memories of our past hopes and dreams. When that happens, we need to look at them again and consider how we might manifest them in reality.

Starter Reading Ilbe is trying to remind you of something you've lost—a hope, perhaps, or a dream. You may have thought it gone forever, but he is holding it out to you for reconsideration. *He* thinks you can do something with it now. The way may not be obvious, but his clever nose has scented a path, a potential opening for bringing this into your life. Sometimes, Ilbe may be saying that a long-awaited dream is at last arriving on the scene and there is nothing we need to do but open our hearts and minds to it. However, we usually have to work for it.

Another attribute of Ilbe is loyalty.

Reverse Is it time to stop saying "I can't" and take a look at "I can" instead? Perhaps something important in your life is being held back by negative attitudes, but we have choices about our attitudes and can change them when they are not helping us.

Alternatively, Ilbe may be saying that this is not yet the time for the germination of *this* seed. It may be that other things need to be dealt with first. What might you need to clear out or finish up before being able to properly plant and nurture this seed? Are the things in the way weeds, which should simply be pulled, or valued growing things that we would wish to care for before planting something new in that space in our lives?

Card 42—Myk the Myomancer

Small clues. Details. The messages everywhere. Patience.

Myk the Myomancer

A myomancer reads the past, present, and potential of all beings in the movements of mice. Myk is particularly fond of reading the movements of field mice, as they are livelier and better fed than church mice. Myk could learn the same things by reading berries or the patterns made by fallen leaves or any one of a billion other things, but his specialty is mice. He can learn endless things from the way they twitch their whiskers and hold their tails. He sees hidden information in the patterns of growth and coloration in their fur, the way the wind rumples it, and how they preen themselves.

Little things can tell us a lot. Everything bears messages about the universe around us. Studying the details sometimes enables us to deduce the whole.

The entire universe is one piece, and each fragment of that one Unity (Card 1) reflects and is connected to all the others. That famous philosopher Anonymous once said, "The lifting of a finger disturbs the farthest star." Myk says it works the other way around, too. He advises us to make a slow and observant study of the little things and their even smaller details in the world around us. He says that such study not only helps us enhance our understanding of life, Unity, and everything, but it also helps to develop a joyful patience and a deeper philosophy.

Starter Reading Attention to details is important at this time. Little things are not only important in themselves, but they also give you important information about larger things. Look for the inner, hidden meaning in ordinary objects, happenings, and experiences. Life is trying to teach you something by speaking to you gently. With luck and application you will get the message before it has to speak to you more loudly.

Body language in humans as well as mice may give you very useful information at this present time, especially if you learn to read it properly.

The clues to the answers you seek and the things you need to know are all around you. You are surrounded by omens, portents, and signs, but the signs are not written on billboards in large letters. They are in the small happenings of your life. Be awake and aware.

Hint: If you work out what the question really is, it is much easier to recognize the answer when it comes.

Reversed Possibly we are ignoring information readily available to us because we think the source is not important enough to pay attention to. Or perhaps we are seeing the messages and denying their validity because we don't like them. These are very human (read "not very wise") things to do.

On the other hand, we might need to realize that, while everything has meanings, not all meanings are worth worrying about. Sometimes it is important to keep the broad picture in mind and avoid getting lost in the detail. If we feel confused by too many details and can't see the storm for the raindrops, we can try backing up and looking at our overall goals and situation.

Card 43—Geeeeeooo the Slooow
Cycles of time. Slowness. Waiting. Patience.

Geeeeeooo is the Gnome of Slow Processes. How long is it going to take for that water to wear that rock away? How much has that mountain grown (or eroded) in the last millennium? Geeeeeooo is there watching attentively, making certain that things don't happen too fast, resulting in a slipshod job. It is he who watches the waves slowly encroach on the shore, wearing away the cliffs. Elsewhere, to keep things in balance, he watches certain mountains slowly grow taller.

Geeeeeooo is also the master of the clarification process whereby we let something sit quietly while the impurities slowly settle themselves out, allowing the substance to purify itself in time.

Geeeeeooo doesn't understand why we rush about so, missing out on the slow changes in the worlds around us. He is amazed at the stress and problems we create for ourselves by doing that. He wonders how we can survive if we don't sit down and watch the sunrises and sunsets or if we "don't have time" to enjoy our lives—especially if we are so busy rushing around with the idea that we are making things good for ourselves *later* but never *now*.

Geeeeooo the Sloooow

The thing about Geeeeeooo's processes is that they all proceed in good order. Fruit ripens on time, grain is ready at harvest time, and the moon and earth circle each other in equitable balance, neither too quickly nor too slowly. These natural processes work well, and in our own lives it is helpful to use them for models, finding the right pace—the pace that allows natural, low-stress growth and progress and joy. The world isn't turning any faster, so we might ask ourselves why we are trying to cram more into our days.

Starter Reading Slow down. Sit back in your chair and think a little. Why are you going so fast? What do you hope to gain from it? Are you metaphorically trying to push the river? What kind of stress is being created in your life by hurrying? The presence of Geeeeeooo in a reading indicates that the situation or issue is part of a long process that cannot well be hurried. It is important to settle in for a long haul and to set a pace that you can maintain for as long as needed, while remaining relaxed and patient. If you are short on patience, try cultivating your acquaintance with the Singer of the Chalice (Card 12). You will find life much more delightful if you do. Geeeeeooo himself clearly does, to judge from his face.

Reverse Unnecessary delays or even stalling may be going on here. Whether the querent is the cause or the victim of this, it may be time for him to give things a tactful but firm push to get them in motion. Geeeeeooo may be in charge of slow processes, but they should be actually proceeding and not stuck.

Lys of the Shadows

Conversely, the reversed Geeeeeooo may have been tumbled over by someone rushing in, unready and unprepared, trying to harvest unripe fruit and likely to only get a stomachache as a result. Set him back on his feet, slow down, and let him proceed at his proper pace.

Card 44—Lys of the Shadows

Healing the shadows. Addictions. Bondage. Self-esteem.

Lys works hard. She has a very tough job to do, and she puts a great deal of tough love into it. She prowls the night streets, looking for those in need of her help—and finds far too many of them.

Lys is the patron faery of social workers, therapists, healers, and all others who try to help alcoholics and drug addicts and other souls caught in the darkness of their own inner shadows or who are abused by those who should have protected them. However, she doesn't sit in an office somewhere—she is out there on the dark and dangerous streets, lending a healing hand here, soothing an anguished brow there, whispering comfort and encouragement into a lonely ear, and bringing a touch of hopeful rainbow light into the deepest shadows, including those in darkened human hearts.

Like *the* Laume (Card 30), much of her work flows through the hearts (and then the hands and words) of humans who make themselves available for such work. She inspires souls to connect with one another in a healing way. Her specialty is help for the hopeless, for the ones that most everyone else (including themselves) has given up on—the street people, the lost children of our society, those who have fallen through the cracks and rips in our feeble social safety nets. Like *the* Laume, she often works through human hands and she may call upon you for help in her work.

Out of curiosity, I asked Lys why she chose to have her card in this particular group of faeries instead of the one before, where I might have expected her to be more at home. She shrugged, gave me a cheeky grin, and said, *"These guys know where to find the best nectar and nuts."* Even though she has wings, our Lys is very down-to-earth and practical.

Starter Reading Ultimately, Lys is trying to help people develop true self-respect and self-esteem, but she has to start much farther down the scale of idealism than that. She tries to inspire practical help for those who need it most. She is the inspiration for the first wobbly steps taken by a damaged soul toward healing. Her presence in a reading indicates that something that had seemed lost and fixed in that loss is now open to healing. Someone is ready to begin, with help, the climb out of the inner mire. There is hope here, and a need for loving kindness tempered by practicality.

If you call upon Lys for assistance in helping another, she will always give it, often by encouraging that person to be receptive and others to also be helpful. She always has time to support those who have time for others.

Reverse Reversed, this card signifies bondage to addictions, compulsive and self-destructive behavior, anger directed toward self (and probably others), and hitting the bottom of the cycle. It may even seem that there is no possible way up. It can also indicate false friends who lead one astray. Separation, loneliness, and isolation are also usually present.

A person may sink to this level because of feelings of guilt. If so, she needs to consider the value of atonement (at one-ment with self) instead of dividing ourselves into judge, criminal, and executioner. It is not always possible to make reparation to those we have hurt, but it *is* always possible to begin working at developing a better balance with the cosmos through action. We can, for example, work to help others who may have been similarly hurt. This takes courage and determination, but through such action self-respect can be regained. The Singers of Courage and Healing are with us if we open ourselves to them. Helping others is one way of opening our hearts.

Taitin the Sylph

Card 45—Taitin the Sylph

Acute intellect. Quickness. Mental synthesis. Discernment.

Taitin glitters and glimmers brightly. She scatters a special faery dust that energizes the mind. However, energy is not everything, and the faery dust that actually makes minds brighter as well as more energized is more rare, and she distributes it much less often. She is full of curiosity and wants to go everywhere, see everything, and have every question answered. Like the two-year-old asking, "Why? Why? Why?" she wants to know all, even the things that by their very nature cannot be known to the conscious mind.

Taitin reminds us that ideas cannot be confined. They are wild and free. They move fast. Some ideas are more contagious than the flu and they move quickly from head to head—sometimes illuminating and sometimes burning out with a flicker and a flash and a faint whiff of ash.

Brian wrote, "The sylph is a fragment of the earth's soul in faery form. In the faery realms, light comes not from above but from within." Like other faeries, sylphs light up the world around them, energizing all who come into contact with them with their quick faery radiance. We humans also light up the world around us with our own auras. It is a pity that so few of us have learned the mental disciplines to be able to perceive that light. However, Taitin is not the one to consult about that—try Laiste (Card 38) or the Dark Lady (Card 20) for that. What Taitin bestows is more ephemeral but nevertheless of value.

She is an awakener, one who startles us into seeing and thinking in new and exciting ways. She loves to sit in on teenage and college-age discussions about the profound questions of life. She is full of bright ideas and willing to discuss them at length. She is not too bothered about whether the discussions make much sense or not. Ideas with wings are her joy, and mental stimulation is her game.

Taitin has inertialess flight; like thought, she is not bound by the rules of mass and momentum. Therefore she can radically change direction without notice, more quickly than a hummingbird.

Starter Reading What we see here is mental quickness, adaptability, and enthusiasm. Ideas and opinions abound. A few are brilliant, but others vary from mediocre to downright silly. Be selective. Mental and psychic abilities may be awakening. Independent thinking is in operation. New ideas and new versions of old ideas are creating an exciting effervescent atmosphere. Avoid excess and extremes. Minds may change often as new ideas and new ways of seeing bubble to the surface.

Out of conflict and confusion, resolved by good will and clear thinking, a new and better understanding may come.

Reverse Fluttery, fickle, fly by night. Reliable? Ha! You *must* be joking. Here we are likely to get into arguments merely for the sake of the excitement and mental fizz of arguing. Petty quarrels can take place. Mental irritability can be a problem. All of this can be rectified if everyone involved makes a conscious effort to become earthed and calm. Mental flights of fancy of the Hummingbird Mind are fun, but until ideas are brought down to Earth, they accomplish nothing.

Card 46—The Friends
Friendship. Support. Aid.

The one on top is Faery Nuff, and I've already told you all that he wants me to say about him in the introduction to Part Two. He and Laochan, his high-speed friend beneath, are the best of friends and can nearly always be found together. Call upon Faery Nuff, and you get Laochan as well. And when you need support or to better understand true friendship, *do* call upon them.

As children, we all have faery playmates and faery guardians. As we grow older, the pressure of parents and others in our community often nag us into blocking our visions of and communications with the faeries. Faery Nuff and Laochan can help us go back to that childlike trust in the faeries and to renew our forgotten friendships with them. They can also often help us to learn more about the true meaning of friendship:

46

The Friends

*Hands outstretched reach across the
rushing water—
you steady me, I steady you on the
slippery rocks
of time. Hands reaching,
giving . . . and giving in return.
I am so grateful to you for being there.
I could never have managed alone.*

Starter Reading Friendly cooperation with others is necessary to reach
mutual goals. Willingness to give and
receive assistance and support is also
required. Ask friends for help and
suggestions, listen with respect, and
accept the gifts willingly offered. Unconditional receiving is even more difficult than unconditional giving. Four
feet are more stable than two.

Alternatively, Faery Nuff and
Laochan may be saying that you will
benefit at this time from offering
support and aid to a friend. Look around you. Someone you love may be
needing your help and be too bound up by fear of rejection or pride to ask.
Volunteer your help to your friends and give unconditionally from a generous, loving heart. It will do you good, increasing your store of credit for
help in time of need, and it might even help them.

Reverse When you stand this card on its head, Faery Nuff gets tangled up
in himself and thinks he is Naught Faery Nuff. Things don't go well then.
There may be spats, misunderstandings, and disagreements. He and his
friend may quarrel over nothing much and rifts may occur. It is time to sort
things out. Call in Honesty and his good friend, Tact. Get things back in
balance and the right way up with serious, loving discussions. Cultivate
your friendships, and plant the seeds for new ones. You need your friends,
so don't let misunderstandings or touchiness (yours or theirs) get in the way.
Reopen your heart to them, and give them reason to reopen their hearts to
you. Like the apostle Paul wrote, "Love is patient and kind."

Card 47—The Oak Men
Strength. Ancient wisdom. Depth.

I had an interesting lesson from the Oak Men about how we humans use faeries to mirror our own projections. The eyes of the Oak Men are a warm light brown, but some people look at them and say, "Ooooh, red eyes! Scary!" I tried a little experiment. Using digital magic, I made a copy of the Oak Men and gave them blue eyes. I then asked some people for their impressions of the Men, and words like "innocent" and "sweet" and "melancholy" came back. Then I changed them to an unreal-looking violet and got responses like, "Oooh, so *spiritual*! So *wise*."

Had the Oak Men changed? Of course not, but what people projected onto them had! When we look at a faery, we can simply project all of our fears and insecurities and prejudices and delusions on them—or we can try to see them as they are. In a sense, all oracles are simply mirrors of the wisdom and confusion within the reader, but if we only look at them through our personal filters and projection, we learn very little. It is only when we actually try to see beyond ourselves that we begin to use the oracle as a mirror of the cosmos and all of its wisdom.

One member of the Oracle group looked at them and wrote, "When I see this card I lose all track of time. I feel *deep* grounding and peace, contentment. Everything is there if you just take the time to be part of it. It is a deep homecoming for me. To me, the Oak Men show the deep wisdom of age, the inner peace and strength of the elders."

This is what the Oak Men are about. Can you look at them and see them as they are, or can you only see your own projections? The universe (like the Oak Men) is full of wisdom and compassion and strength, but it doesn't always come in pretty packages.

Starter Reading This card depicts the strength and wisdom of age. It also reminds us that what we need to know, what is truly there to be seen, cannot be discovered by a superficial glance and hasty reaction. In a reading, the Oak Men tell us to look slowly and deeply into the heart of the matter and to see past the superficialities of the surface. Consider the history of the situation in depth, and learn from the past. Consult others with more experience than you have. Learn from the wisdom of the elders, both those available to you personally and those you encounter in books and elsewhere. In this matter it would be wise to make your decisions after more pondering and study of the situation. Consider motivations in depth. Take action only after thorough deliberation. The Oak Men tell us that haste may be, at this moment, our worst enemy.

They also suggest that we might learn a lot from trees. Consider the trees and their wisdom. Connect with a wise old one and ask for help.

Reverse Turn the Oak Men upside down and you see different faces with other expressions. The Oak Men wish you to use your own perceptiveness and intuition in working out what they are saying in this position. This is not a trick—it is just a little exercise in stretching yourself and your vision. Enjoy!

"Fairies speak to us in many, many ways and we perceive their intent with our ears, our eyes, and our hearts and our laughter too."

—Brian

Card 48—A Collective of Pixies

Duty. Willingness. Joyful participation. Virtue

A pixie's gotta do what a pixie's gotta do, and one of the things a pixie has to do is to dance. It *has* to be done, so that the flowers will grow and fruit, the grass will do its photosynthesis thing, the trees will put down their roots properly, and other processes will proceed in their proper time, at their

proper pace. The pressure of the pixies' energetic little etheric feet may
even be what helps to keep the world
turning at the right speed—at least,
they claim it does. (I know that physicists claim differently, but who would
you rather believe? Besides, physicists
keep changing their minds about
things, and pixies have done this
dance *forever* and the world has kept
on turning, hasn't it? All the physicists
do, anyway, is to explain how the pixies' dance *works*, not who does it.)

A Collective of Pixies

Approaching these tasks with
lightheartedness is, they say, essential.
It lends virtue (in the sense of *potency*)
to their actions. Otherwise, their feet
would come down too heavily and
stunt the growth of things instead of
enhancing it—or they might step too
lightly, and then things might grow
the wrong way up or sideways. It
could make the world turn wrong.

Pixies could treat their duty as something boring or oppressive, but
they *choose* to take joy in doing it and doing it well. Are you faced with duties? Like the old saying goes, a merry heart makes light work. We have a
choice about how we do anything. We can make a game of it and do it happily. We can take an attitude that makes it demanding and oppressive. We
can choose to regard it as boring and dull. When we choose the first attitude, the results have a different feeling, a different energy than the results
of the other two. Anyone and everything that come in contact with the results of that work feels the difference and is affected differently by it,
whether they notice it or not. So, here is another of those places where we
can make the world better or worse—and do the same to ourselves simultaneously.

Starter Reading What is needed here is not only an awareness of duty but
a merry approach to it. This job has to be done, so one might as well do it

willingly. Progress through this dance maze step by step—*lithely and lightly.* Take joy and pride in achievement. Approach the work with zeal, zest, and zing—and perhaps even a little zaniness as well. Otherwise, you might as well not bother—well, *almost.* There is something about this lighthearted approach to your duty that is important at this time in order to achieve the results you want.

Additionally, consider the words *collective* and *cooperative* as you make your plans. This situation may take more than one person, perhaps several working together to achieve the desired results. Joining forces with others is appropriate at this time. Seek the cooperation of friends, family, coworkers, and faeries, as appropriate.

Reverse When pixies haven't enough to do, they tend to get into mischief together. They decide they *ought* to lead the travelers astray, chase the farmer's cows from the field, tangle the computer's wires and tickle its memory, and cross the telephone lines. Make sure that everyone involved knows what they are expected to do here and that they have enough work to keep them busy without being overloaded.

Alternatively, some people may be dragging their feet, not getting their job done, promising and then not delivering. Invite them to join the dance. If possible, help them to see the joy and satisfaction to be found in doing a good job cheerfully. Set a good example.

Card 49—Mikle à Muckle
Everyday blessings. Play. Mixed blessings.

Mikle à Muckle (aka A Mixed Blessing) is a grig of good family. As you have doubtless heard, grigs are merry—so merry that they have become proverbial for it. They want you to be merry too, with a childlike open heart. Mikle informs us, *"Little things come in good packages."* He is a little thing, and therefore is good and well packaged in his skin. This is faery logic, and I'm not responsible for it.

Mikle can be foolish, silly, playful, and absurd. He is fond of goofing off and considers play to be an art form and himself a fine artist. He understands renewing the spirit and re-creating the body and emotions. He knows that all of us have a child within who needs to play and be cherished. He also knows we need to make mistakes so we can learn from them, which is how he got the title of A Mixed Blessing.

When we stop pretending to be adults for a moment, stop trying to live up to some impossible and probably boring standard, we can regain the clear, direct vision of a child. We can, like Mikle, see things as they really are, and we can focus on the present moment, which is our only place of power. Here and now is where we can do things, change things, and enjoy *real* things instead of mere ideas and dreams. Mikle reminds us that the past is past, gone forever, the future is just a dream, and *now* is the *only* time we have, moment by moment.

Mikle is a great adventurer, an explorer of life. He leads us to hidden, surprising, magical places if we let him.

Starter Reading Lighten up! What is needed here is the benefit of a childlike, trusting heart and childlike wisdom, seeing directly into the true nature of things. Don't complicate matters. What you see is what you get. Don't look for hidden and subtle meanings and motivations because they are not there in this case. Go to the heart of the matter, the simple core hidden behind complexities. Don't be so caught up in thinking about the future that you can't see what is happening *now*.

Welcome adventure into your life. Try something you've never done before.

And take some time to play with Mikle before you turn into a grumpy glumph or a worn-out wurg.

Reverse This card reversed can signify behavior that is opportunistic, self-centered, inconsiderate, selfish, and childish. Immature, too. It can speak of clinging to unrealistic notions about security, clinging to the known path, rejecting adventure. *"Don't,"* Mikle says, *"let yourself do that! Please!"*

Arval Parrot

Card 50—Arval Parrot
Communication.

Arval points to the light in his throat center. In esoteric lore, the energy center at the throat is about communication. Faeries are great communicators, though not necessarily in words as we use them. They speak through words, of course, but they also speak through the rustle of leaves, the pattern of clouds in the sky, the way flower petals fall. They tickle us with touches almost too subtle to feel, trying to get our attention, and they sometimes speak through our dreams and daydreams. Their communications are something like those of cats—part verbal, part body language, part telepathy, and part pure faery.

Arval says that we humans can semaphore each other by flashing the lights in our throat centers. In fact, he says we *do* that, and read the messages on an unconscious level, which is one of the ways we pick up on the unspoken feelings and thoughts of each other.

Arval also says—and I agree—that almost any situation can be improved by people *listening* to each other, and that listening is a full half of good communication. The other half, of course, is speaking truly and clearly. Some people use speech as a game or as a test for others to see if they can puzzle out the meaning, and this is faerily fun as long as actual communication doesn't matter. When it does, though, it is helpful if we try for clarity, at the very least, and hopefully wisdom as well.

Arval has many wise sayings to help us. *"It takes two to say 'yes' but only one to say 'no'. Where the stream is shallowest, greatest is the noise. He that always complains is never pitied. Better than gold is a tale rightly told. 'Tis easier to give advice than to take it. From the place where deer are not, they're not easy to be got. Whoever burns his bottom must himself sit on it."*

Well. Enough of *that*.

Arval reminds us that good clear communication is sometimes hard work. It requires elbow grease because the elbows are the secondary energy centers to the throat. He wishes you to know that his elbows are well greased.

Starter Reading Clear communications are vitally important here. Strive for verbal brilliance. Listen carefully. Be articulate. Be willing to calmly debate the issues and explore ideas with others. Open communication will enhance the chances of success all around. Arval also suggests that the querent watch for body language, incomplete sentences, and unfinished thoughts, and try to discover what these signals are meant to get across.

Reversed Communications are blocked. Messages may be going astray. Confusion is 70 percent likely—and rising. Double-check whenever possible. If you just heard someone say something out of character, it may be well that you misheard or misunderstood. There may be missing e-mail, post gone astray, or important words unsaid. Someone may have laryngitis, his throat blocked by unspoken words. Useful information held in silence benefits no one and may harm the situation.

Card 51 – The Topsie-Turvets
Change of viewpoint. Fresh looks. New ways of seeing.

When life is confusing, the Turvets may come to visit you. Nothing draws them like a bit of mental muddle. They don't cause our disarray (we are very good at doing that for ourselves and each other), but they are attracted to it. Confusion is an important stage of growth, and they delight in helping things to grow. They live everywhere (not only humans need their help) and are exceedingly busy. Fortunately, they are quite prolific, so there are a lot of them.

When the Topsie-Turvets show up, it indicates that someone needs to look again, to make an effort to see things from a different point of view. It suggests that confusion may exist because we are asking the wrong questions. Or perhaps we have made assumptions that are incorrect, and we have run into a brick wall built of those misconceptions. The Turvets ask us to back up, to question our assumptions, and to try to see things from the

The Topsie Turvets

51

viewpoints of the other people involved in our muddle. They ask us to let go of our attachment to our own point of view, to stop saying "ought" and "should"—especially about other people. Most emphatically they suggest that we start trying to see things as they really are instead of as someone thinks they should be. This card is a warning that someone involved in the question or issue at hand is mentally upside down. Or possibly sideways.

Starter Reading In a reading, the Turvets suggest that things need to be looked at from another angle. We need to back off from our emotional entanglement and look anew. Much of the apparent confusion about the issue is caused by a faulty point of view. Get the opinions of honest others and then re-look at your own. Defensiveness and denial may be causing much difficulty. Try imagining that you are looking at the situation from the point of view of each of the others involved. This is not an exercise in deciding how the other "ought" to see things, but in discovering how they really do. Words like "he ought to see that . . ." are not useful at this time.

   If the Turvets' card turns up and another point of view does not readily suggest itself, it may be useful to draw another card for further information. Or you might choose to do another reading, addressing that issue independently. Remember to pause to listen for hints from the Turvets themselves. They are the experts in the field.

"I believe no faery is completely good or bad but fluidly embodies both extremes."

—Brian

Reversed This card is always reversed, even when it is turned sideways in a layout. *"Only worse,"* the Turvets say glumly.

Card 52 – The Rarr
Wild energy. Pure potential.

Once upon a time there were three pink boys (more or less) and a Rarr, who all played in Brian's son Toby's bedroom. They liked the midnight tea parties, the magical ambience, and of course, they liked Toby. Unfortunately, the Pink Boys got too rowdy, and Brian had to throw them out into the garden, which was where they belonged anyway. The Rarr learned from the experience, in a rarrish way, and it quieted down a bit during the midnight hours.

Rarrs are not naughty or wicked, just energetic. They are also not very discriminating. They like to join into whatever excitement is going on and add energy to it. In a way, they are pure potential, and they potentize whatever is happening. Rarrs are attracted to mobs rioting and to meditation groups rising toward ecstasy and to any other strong energy states.

Rarrs are a bit like Tigger in the Pooh stories. They bounce; they zoom; they go off on wild tangents. (Brian hasn't painted a Wild Tangent yet, as far as I know, but I know what they look like, having encountered more than my share!)

Think of the *rrrarr* of a growling dog, the *rrrarr* of an engine revving up, the *rrrr* of a purring cat, and the *arrr* in Arrrugh! As I say, Rarrs don't discriminate. It is up to us to do that. They put a live spark into whatever is happening. It is our choice what we do with it.

Starter Reading A Rarr in your cards encourages you to be especially attentive to what you are doing with your energy and intentions. Don't get carried away by the Rarr's bouncy enthusiasm, but do take advantage of the energy. You can accomplish a great deal with the energy being made available to you. This is a good time. Note that the Rarr is not grounded—and is not meant to be—but humans need to keep their feet firmly on the earth. When you encounter the Rarr, breathe slowly. Center. Earth yourself. Be clear about your objectives and then go for them.

Reversed The Rarr upside down indicates a terrible problem. Both the querent and the Rarr are losing (or have lost) control and are thrashing about in midair. Faery glamour and faery zaps are running wild. Illusions and delusions are rife. Misunderstandings escalate. A cold shower is definitely in order. Practice grounding exercises. Meditate. Back off and look at things coolly. This may not be enough, but please try.

The Faery Challengers

The Faery Challengers bring us face to face with our fears, our denials, our inner traumas, our insecurities, our delusions and confusions, and our misbehaviors. These are the faeries who, metaphorically speaking, stick out a foot in front of us to see if we are paying attention to where we are going. They test our alertness and awareness, our insight, our knowledge, our wisdom, and our dedication to our personal growth. Without them, we might get very lazy.

Faery tests and challenges are not like the tests we had in school, which only discovered what we had already learned. They design their tests so that, in the process of passing them, we actually learn things that move us up to a higher level of being. They also do not offer us these challenges unless they feel we have the potential of passing. In other words, these are not mere tests but initiations. Some are minor, some are major.

What people often don't realize, when we are blaming the faeries for our own errors, is that the faeries earnestly hope that we will pass our tests, preferably on the first go. Otherwise, they have to administer them again and again. These are terrible jobs, but someone has to do them. They would much prefer to be joining in faery dances or lazing in the moonlight. They wish you faery good luck and look forward to congratulating you on succeeding with your challenges.

Card 53–Death

Natural, timely endings. Release. Liberation.

Scary, eh? Before you panic, let's remember that if it were not for Death and her hard work, we would all be up to our ears in alligators, mayflies, each other, and just about everything else. Without her to clear the world, there would be no room for growth or new life. This applies to all the realms—physical, mental, emotional, spiritual, and other.

The Death card in all oracles—faery, tarot, and other—does not usually signify actual physical death. In fact, that is rarely the meaning. Rather it indicates a significant change, one that involves letting go of the old life in order to move forward into the new. What we really fear about death is the unknown, the "what next?" of it all. We may be experiencing great pain as a result of holding on to aspects of life that we have outgrown, but humans tend to hold on anyway because we don't *know* what is next. We want guarantees, and instead we get open doors into unknown, darkened spaces. Yet, when we go through these doors, closing them behind us, we discover a whole new world—one in which we can grow and develop into more of what we have the potential of being.

So, here we see Death, her face hidden, without form, holding a dark crystal ball. She herself cannot herself see the future.

Starter Reading Something has reached a natural ending, and there is substantial and irrevocable change in the works. This change may be inner or outer or, most likely, both. It is timely and natural, but there may be much resistance to it. Leaves fall every autumn; in the spring the trees are green again with new leaves. Make room for the new in your life—let the old go, lovingly, gently, willingly.

Reversed Important change is being blocked or delayed by clinging to old habits or things, and therefore the changes that need to happen appear to be difficult and forced upon us. Yet, releasing these outgrown and outworn ways of being *must* happen in order to move into the next stage of development. Meditating upon breathing in truth and breathing out not-truth may be helpful. (Not-truth may be false information or it may be simply confusion or muddle. We don't have to know what it is or look at it; we just need to exhale the *energy* of not-truth.)

It is important to look to the future, however unknown or frightening, rather than trying to tug the past along with us. It may seem impossibly difficult, but the only way to reduce the pain of this process is to step forward into the future willingly.

Card 54—Epona's Wild Daughter
Inner shadows. Nightmare. Depression. Madness. Growth.

In the bleakest part of the night, Dorcha comes, wearing her crown of faery stars. She kneels on the ancient owl, bearer of the hidden wisdom of the night, and, facing into the past with a clear, unflinching gaze, she holds us. We are held immobile, inwardly focused, by her comforting yet implacable light-filled hands. She asks riddles that often seem impossible to answer at first—and yet she will not let us go until we find the solutions within ourselves. She is one of the great teachers of Faery, but her method of teaching makes Socrates' questions look like child's play. We must expect this of Dorcha because her lessons are about the shadow side of ourselves—the things we fear, our insecurities, self-doubts, and denials. She is a practitioner of "tough love" therapy.

Dorcha is the Wild Daughter of Epona, Lady of the Horse and the Moon, and she takes us through the dark, hidden side of ourselves and into healing and fulfillment. From the temporary madness of rage, premenstrual tension, or great stress to the deeper and longer psychoses, she drives us on the journey though our internal hells. When we complete the journey, we are transfigured and transformed, transcending our old selves. We can never be frightened by *that* darkness again, whether our own or that of others. But until that journey is fully complete, we exist in a state of vulnerability—

which is where most of us are most of the time.

Notice, please, that it is she and not her more gentle sister, Laiste, who wears the crown of stars—a mark of service, compassion, and great wisdom. Dorcha's element is moonlight, the fifth element, which tempers and tests the spirit. Through her teaching our inner conflicts and struggles become, as they are resolved, our greatest strengths.

Starter Reading Epona's Wild Daughter, Dorcha, is the sphinx, whose riddles must be answered lest we otherwise be destroyed by our own internal conflicts. Dorcha reminds us that we cannot go forward until we have faced something buried within us that is holding us back. Her presence in a reading tells us that finding and working through this is a task of some urgency. We can expect help in this from other people, from the faeries, and from our dreams, but we must be open to these difficult questions and answers and be ready to face things about ourselves that are not as we would wish them to be. She urges us to heal the unresolved issues about who we *really* are and what we *truly* want to be. This is part of the required course in Self-Transformation 101 that we are all enrolled in here on Planet Earth.

The answers to her riddles often come in a sudden burst of enlightenment, like the "solution" to a Zen koan. We may watch a leaf fall or catch a glimpse of the tiny sliver of the new moon in the sky and suddenly be hit by the answer. Before that happens, we usually work long and hard upon the question, searching and digging for an answer. The realization, when we really have it, will be transformative; we will no longer be the people that we once were.

You don't like this interpretation? Well, I *have* been telling you all along that we (you and I and everyone else) will all receive varying mes-

Epona's Wild Daughter

sages from the faeries in the cards. Yours may well differ from mine. Ask Dorcha what message she has for you—and don't be surprised if her answer is another question or riddle. She and I both wish you well in solving it, with all our hearts.

Reversed This meaning is much the same as above, but it may take longer and the resolution of the issue may be buried more deeply. At this point, the wise person prays for guidance and actively seeks it. I know, I know—that's why we're reading the cards. Yet the presence of Epona's Wild Daughter implies that the answers we truly need are to be found deeply within ourselves. What do our nightmares tell us?

Card 55—The Soul Shrinker
Cruelty. Malice. Gossip. Curses. Destruction. Blessing.

The distasteful task of the Soul Shrinker is to observe what we say to and about others, especially the mean, nasty, and unnecessarily critical things. By observing our behavior this way, he reflects it back to us, making us more aware of it. This is a boddhisattva (a spiritual being devoted to helping to bring about the enlightenment of all) type of job, and it requires great compassion, understanding, and forgiveness if the Soul Shinker himself is not to be dragged down to our level. If we are just inwardly spluttering, looking for words, he may even suggest to us the words that express our feelings and energy. Then it is our choice—our test—whether or not we say them.

There are two important things about malicious gossip, unnecessary criticism, verbal cruelty, sarcasm, and "scoring off" of others. One is that it demeans the speaker, makes him less, makes his aura darker, and encourages the behavior as a habit, continually eroding the brightness and potential goodness of the speaker. The other important thing is that this is a way that *we actually curse others*.

Even if the recipient doesn't hear the actual words of the blessing or curse, even if the words are not spoken aloud, they are carried as discordant notes through Ekstasis's (Card 2) song of the universe to the recipient. Fortunately, that is not all there is to it or such behavior would be unforgivably wicked—not that it isn't pretty nearly that anyway. We all have a choice about whether we accept curses or blessings.

If we choose not to accept it, then all of the energy boomerangs back to the sender, who then gets a well-deserved double dose of it.

Once, long ago, the Soul Shrinker was very beautiful, but listening to and witnessing all of this human ugliness has rubbed off on his appearance, like that of a lovely frog in a polluted pool with his skin raw and forming hideous growths. His heart is compassionate and anguished; his heartfelt wish is that we learn "right speech" and "right thought." Every wicked thing a human says makes the Soul Shrinker more ugly. Every time a human learns this lesson, the Soul Shrinker becomes a bit less ugly. As you can see, humanity as a whole has a *lot* of work to do on this.

The Soul Shrinker

Starter Reading Critical and malicious thoughts and words are having a detrimental effect on the situation and the people involved in it. Steps need to be taken to banish this curse energy through love and compassion—or at the very least, through forgiveness and a refusal to accept the curse into oneself. Understanding the implications of this and transforming the behavior and feelings involved is a major and often very difficult step in human spiritual development.

One of the things usually involved here is taking responsibility for ourselves and our own feelings rather than blaming others for the way we are. Another part of this process is to learn to be compassionate toward ourselves. If we can do that, it is much easier not to be horrible to and about others.

This doesn't mean that we are supposed to be all sweetness and light all the time. Constructive criticism, given compassionately, is a part of being *real*—and *reality* is a good thing to be in touch with.

Reverse Malice, vicious gossip, and cruelty are occurring somewhere in this situation, cursing the people involved. The best way to change this is to begin scattering blessings, thank-yous, positive feedback, and kind words in

56

Gloominous Doom

all directions. It helps a lot if they are actually *meant*.

Card 56 – Gloominous Doom

Self-defeat. Self-pity. Self-destruction. Taking care of ourselves.

Self-pity is the first step on the slippery, seductive slide toward self-destruction.

Much of what I've said above about the Soul Shrinker (Card 55) applies to Gloominous Doom, so please read about the Soul Shrinker first. It may seem odd to have such a seemingly lightweight Challenger as Gloominous Doom right next to the Soul Shrinker, but they are the closest of cousins. The Soul Shrinker observes the way we curse others, through energy and attitude; Gloominous Doom observes the way we curse ourselves.

In a way, thought, the part of ourselves that he witnesses is *worse* than what the Soul Shrinker sees. When we curse others through sending the energy of malice and ill will toward them, they may reject our sendings. However, when we curse ourselves through self-pity and self-destructive attitudes, there is little, if any, resistance, and the curse takes immediate effect—and continues to act until we change our attitudes.

It's interesting, isn't it, how we can see at once that the Soul Shrinker is ugly, but Gloominous Doom has a certain charm, a kind of weird attractiveness. We feel sorry for him! He looks so pitiful. And there *is* another side to him that one Oracle group participant sees. "I feel that Gloominous Doom is underrated as a helper. He can be there for you when no one else wants to know. The state of self-pity, when all seems terrible, and the whole world is against you, is an important part of the process. We all get down sometimes. You could say that we even need it to compare with when we feel good.

"Gloominous Doom is ready and willing to help us explore just how awful it all feels, just how bad it is, and how hard done by we feel—and what has made us feel like that in the first place. It is very important to really get to know these feelings—or how can you possibly let them go if you don't properly know them in the first place? Our feelings need to be fully acknowledged and understood, or we just tuck them away and hide them from sight—until they appear again, maybe in a different guise.

"Gloominous Doom helps us properly explore our gloomy feelings of doom so that we can be done with them. It is a very important job."

The ultimate test here, of course, is to take responsibility for ourselves and our attitudes and to choose a path that is life-affirming, not life-denying. The sorrier we feel for ourselves, the worse our life becomes. Reread that last sentence, please! *It is* not *the other way around.* Self-pity makes things worse, and we have a choice, one we have every moment, as to whether we want to make our lives better or worse. And only we can choose that for ourselves.

Starter Reading It is time to face the fact that our attitudes and beliefs about ourselves are our own. We may have learned them from others, but the others are not responsible for them in the here and now. We are. If we choose self-pity and pessimism, we make a choice that makes our lives worse. When this card appears in a reading, it indicates that this is a time when understanding that concept is especially important—a time when there is some sort of a crunch in the situation that offers someone the opportunity to notice and change such self-destructive habits. If it is yourself, you know what you need to do. If it is someone else, you may wish to consider how you might support them in this opportunity for change. Can you make sure to give positive feedback at every appropriate opportunity? Can you refrain from nagging, scolding, or complaining at them when they get it wrong? These things help.

Reversed Someone is sunk in self-pity, and this is having a deleterious effect on that person and on the situation. I hate to say it, but there is very little anyone but that person can do to change the attitude. It is important to remember that trying to push someone else into a different attitude usually only encourages them to resist us, making matters worse. (See the Soul Shrinker, Card 55.) Take this into account in making your own plans and decisions, and get on with doing the best you can with your life. It is up to the other person to sort out her own attitudes.

An Oracle reader from our on-line group shows a way that we can deal with excessive self-pity in ourselves by meeting our own needs and desires for comforting. She says, "I have a pity party when I'm feeling down. I give myself permission to enjoy this feeling to the nth degree. I wallow in it. I get all of the junk food I can think of, rent the worst (really groan) movies, get my blankie, and I'm set. Pretty soon, I can't remember why I was down, but I sure had a great time while it lasted. I highly recommend it."

"In modern life we are not free from the plagues and torments of bad faeries. They make their presence known to us through all manner of disruptions, from minor daily irritations to serious problems affecting our health and well-being."

—Brian

Card 57—Luathas the Wild
Haste. Impulsiveness. Fire. Spontaneity. Balance.

Luathas the Wild is filled with fire, and fire is associated with the creative life force. This faery fires us up, gets us going, recharges our batteries and creative energies. He likes to be around when things are exciting, when there is life force blazing high and he can jump in and encourage it to burn even higher. Creation and passion are his bailiwick. *"Faster! Faster! Faster!"* is his motto. A waitress serving me breakfast, looked over my shoulder as she rushed past and paused on her toes as she saw Luathas. "Ohhh!" she exclaimed, balancing three full plates and two coffee pots, "He looks like a *bad* faery. I don't want him in *my* life!" Then she took off at a near run for the people down the aisle, who were gesturing for coffee.

We have to be careful with Luathas. He doesn't know the meaning of words like *slow, stop, rest, respite, catnap, moderation, gradual, pace, gentle, ease, peace.* These are all things that humans must know in order to live creatively and constructively with him. Anything else is fatal, sooner or later—and probably sooner at that.

The fire of Luathas can be destructive as well as creative. Rage, fury, and anger are all part of the fire element as well. Fire burns as well as energizes. Think of the gentle warmth of a full and sleeping kitten, its inner fire converting milk to bone and muscle and to extravagant friskiness; or the flame of the candle, lighting the wanderer's way home; or the anger of a hurt soul, lashing out at others; or the inferno of a forest fire, wild and overpowering.

57

Luathas the Wild

Creation and destruction are inextricably linked. The fire that burns creates ash, which in turn acts as fertilizer for new growth. The slopes of volcanoes are highly fertile, which is why people take the risk of living and farming on them.

Think of the Phoenix, who lays her egg and then bursts into flame to incubate it. Birth, death, and rebirth are the cycle of fire.

Starter Reading This card says that wild creative energies are being brought to whatever position it represents in the card layout. It often fires up the things that surround it (represented by other cards), energizing them as well. It tells us that it is important to think and act creatively, and it says that the energy to do so is available. New approaches are called for here. Old ideas and old behaviors will not do it. Sometimes it may be useful to draw another card (or do an additional layout) to get some suggestions about what those new ideas might be.

Alternatively, Luathas may be telling you to go for something—*now!* For example, another member of our Oracle discussion group was at a convention and a man was demonstrating electronic devices. She was not particularly interested in them, but he and she talked about the different meters and tools for a while. She started to walk away and then she thought, "No, I've got to do this." She went back and told him, "I don't think I'll ever forgive myself if I don't tell you, I think I'm in love with you." They've been happily married for many years now.

Sometimes it is important to take the risk of making a fool of yourself to gain something amazing and wonderful and miraculous. Sometimes, when Luathas says, *"Go for it! Now!"* it is important to do so. And sometimes it isn't. If the only reason for caution is that you're afraid of looking silly, it probably *is* time to go for it.

Remember, then, that you need to keep an eye on Luathas. Don't let him have control of your schedule or the accelerator in your car. He always thinks going faster and taking chances is better, and sometimes he is even right. Use sense and stay grounded, even while he takes you off on a flight of fancy.

Reversed In a reversed position, Luathas speaks of burnout—blocked or even exhausted creative energy. He suggests that we need to find ways to regenerate and recharge ourselves so we can continue the race, but at our own healthy pace. He suggests that our fire is low and must be replenished by appropriate activities before we can resolve the issues we are dealing with.

Here we see the reversed Luathas representing fire in its destructive mode, however grim or delightful that process may appear to be. We must remember that destruction is not always a bad thing. There are things that need to be destroyed—injustice and cruelty, for example— but these things have to be handled with great care. We cannot heal injustice with more injustice, nor cruelty with additional cruelty. If we wish to fight the twisted fire of cruelty (which is passion gone sour and insane), we must find a way to lovingly counter it with the fire of creativity and compassion.

Luathas is eager to help with his wonderful creative, destructive fire, but we must be careful with him. He is the epitome of unbounded enthusiasm and can lead us to burnout or to glory. We must use his fire well or he will take control and use us, leaving nothing but a little pile of ashes blowing away in the wind.

Ffaff the Ffooter

Card 58—Ffaff the Ffooter

Being Real. Earthing. Grounding. Centering.

Just as life is becoming surprising, exciting, and very interesting (though not necessarily fun), Ffaff the Ffoot Ffungus Ffaery comes along to check out our feet. He picks up one foot in his remarkably strong hands and looks it over for ffluff between the toes, smelly ffungi, and dirty, untrimmed toenails. If he finds any of these signs of disrespect for our feet and for Earthmama (walking on her with grubby ffeet, yuk!), he marks them by making holes in our socks. If things are really bad, he sends mice to eat our dancing shoes so we will be forced to dance barefoot in the dewy meadows under the moon. If it happens that we have snow instead of dew, that is just our tough luck.

(Warning: Ffaff may have fungi on his fingers from someone else's foot, and if our feet are not clean, both energetically *and* physically, the fungi are apt to take root.)

He leaves that foot in the air while he inspects the other foot, lifting it up as well. Having done his inspection job, he wanders off, leaving us standing there with both ffeet in the air. *"And,"* Ffaff snickers, *"usually, conffused expreffion on your ffaces."*

This is not a good position for a human to be in. This is a test. Repeat: This is a test! You have been warned. The test is to get both ffeet, excuse me, feet back on terra firma. Do not try to do anything important or make any significant decisions until you have come back to Earth. Anything you attempt to do while standing with your feet in the air is apt to not work—if you are lucky. If you are unlucky, it will work—but not at all in the way you intend or hope.

Quick Faery Tips for Earthing

Stroke your feet gently with both hands, each one for five minutes. You can also check for holes in your socks while doing this.

Paint your toenails bright red; then your toes say a cherry (or should that be *cheery?*) "Heya!" to you when you look at them, and this reminds you to keep them on the ground. Even when you can't see them, it will probably still remind you, especially if you are a man.

Starter Reading Breathe. Ground. Center. (If you can't remember how, read "Preparing for a Reading," starting on page 181.) Maintain (or recover) sanity by staying earthed. Do this now! Important information is coming your way, but you can only receive it properly if your feet are on terra firma and your head is well connected to the rest of your body.

Reversed Oh, help! Get someone to send a balloon up and pull you back down to Earth with it. This is urgent. It is difficult, sometimes impossible, to contact you from Planet Earth while you are floating off in your own personal soap bubble. Do come back. Do this right now! The world is full of sharp edges for soap bubbles to run into; then they go *pop!* and tumble us onto the hard ground or into dark and dangerous waters below. The better choice is to bring our own selves down gently into the embrace of Earthmother.

Alternatively, learn to fly properly.

This card reversed can also speak of those who draw their energy from others rather than from the source, Ekstasis's song (Card 2), having lost awareness of that fundamental connection. It can indicate that we have lost a proper sense of ourselves as whole and holy and are seeing ourselves as much less than we are.

"The transformative power of Faery turns muck into magic, dross into shining gold, black despair into crystalline joy. As life grows out of death, good can grow from all things we call bad."

—Brian

Card 59 – The Bodacious Bodach

**Meddling. Tampering. Sabotage.
"Helpful fixing." Order.**

The Bodacious Bodach

The Bodach (or Old Man, in Scots
Gaelic) means well. He likes to "fix"
things. He drops down chimneys at
night and tidies up for you. If you
don't have a chimney, he'll find another way in. You left a stack of papers
on your desk? He'll file them for
you—probably in someone else's
desk. No one put away the uneaten
roast beef? He'll assume you don't
want it and give it to the neighbor's dog.

He is not the faery who ties
elf-locks in you hair and makes bits of
it stand out in odd directions while
you sleep. That is just a cousin of his;
he has far more important work to do.

The Bodach is a meddler. He will tell you, if you catch him, that he
means well.

It's just that things never turn out quite as he expects them to. He
feels that you should be grateful for his so-called help (even while you clean
the metaphorical eggs off of the metaphorical walls), and he is amazed when
you are not. Although his feelings are easily hurt by your lack of apprecia-
tion, he is persistent. He will just redouble his efforts to be helpful. The
only way to discourage him is to tidy up your own loose ends and clutter.

I'm sure you know people like the Bodach. They helpfully answer
your phone and take down the wrong message—then they lose it and give
you a garbled verbal version. Worse yet, they give other people messages
from you that are not exactly (or even nearly) what you said. On the rare
occasion that they do pass something on accurately, it is either something
you never meant to pass on or it is said specifically to the wrong person.
The Bodach also likes to gossip.

The Bodach used to steal naughty children but has evidently decided they are not worth having. However, he does pinch them in their sleep sometimes and give them nightmares.

It is said that one can keep him away by putting salt on the hearth, but don't you believe it. He is like an ant—the only way to really keep him away is to not have anything around that might attract him. Tidy up your clutter—physical, mental, and emotional.

Starter Reading Someone somewhere is meddling uninvited in the issue. It may be you, it may be someone else. See if you can work out who it is and begin to untangle the messy web they have woven of confusion and disorder and misunderstanding (so much worse than our own natural disorder). It will take great firmness to get this person to keep his sticky fingers out of your affairs (or you to keep yours out of the affairs of others). The amount of tact you use in sorting this out is up to you, but the Bodach-type person doesn't usually notice hints. Remember, whoever it is *says* they mean well. They may even believe that. It is very hard to believe that the Bodach's bad results are always "just an accident," as he insists. He may believe this, but we don't have to. The word *sabotage* comes to mind. If you don't want the Bodach hanging around looking for ways to help, make sure you don't leave things in the wrong place or dangle any loose ends; he might find some bodacious things to do with them.

Reverse Actually, the Bodach is one of the brownies, who mostly are helpful little spirits around the house. Every little once in a while, his essential brownie nature breaks through and he does truly helpful things. When he does this, reward him—or whoever it is in your life who normally gets it wrong and just this once has got it right. Gratitude and praise are in order. Maybe he'll even get it right next time, too.

Card 60 —The Pook
Shape-changer. Good in bad; bad in good. Paradox. Resolution.

The Pook is a shape-changer. He appears in whatever guise he thinks will be most confusing to you, depending on his purpose. Brian wrote, "He weaves spells to bemuse our senses and confuse our judgment. He is a master of the arts of illusion and delusion, holding up a distorting mirror to reveal the bad in the good and the good in the bad."

The Pook also wishes to show us the "bad" in what we think to be "good" and vice versa. This may confuse us further, or it may help us to gain a more balanced understanding of *how things really are*. He is very against rigid mind-sets and, in his own way, encourages the development of inquiring minds.

His true face? I'm not certain that a shape-changer even has a true face—though he did hold still long enough for Brian to paint him. However, the Pook is very proud of the faces he assumes. With them, he offers us contradictions and paradoxes, and finds it all too easy to confuse our judgment because we are often not thinking very clearly anyway. Sometimes we even hold two or more contradictory beliefs in boxes in our minds. If one is true, we think when we finally consider them, then the other must be false. Not so. Perhaps both are false; perhaps both are partly true and partly false. We tend to cling desperately to our beliefs, even when they make no sense to others or are counter to our actual experience.

60

The Pook

Our paradoxes and confusions are self-created, and the Pook need only dress them up a bit, add a little sparkle, and dangle them before us in order to induce confusion. In that confusion, we are likely to believe almost anything someone presents to us, just to feel as if we have a metaphorical anchor in reality. His challenge for us is to *wake up*, to stop projecting our confusions on reality. Once we have seen the truth, seeming contradictions and paradoxes melt away, in the manner of realizing the solution to a Zen koan like, "What is the sound of one hand clapping?"

When we get the answer, usually by a burst of insight cutting through the confusion and paradoxes, it always seems so simple and we wonder how we could have been in such a tizzy about so simple a thing. We wonder why everyone doesn't understand this so very obvious thing.

Starter Reading It is time for the resolution of seeming contradictions and paradoxes in the situation. Someone or some part of the situation is cloaked in confusion, and our muddled thoughts must be stripped away, revealing truth. We just need to think about it; the information we needed is now available to us. And as soon as we have that burst of insight and *get it*, it's time for us to make changes based on our newly clear understanding.

Alternatively, it may be time for us to make a reality check on the good/bad labels we put on things. Make a list of the "good" (possibly even surprising things) about this situation, and another list about the "bad" ones. If you are not in the habit of seeing the good in the bad and the bad in the good, having preferred a black-and-white world rather than one with colors, you may need some help in learning to do this well.

Reversed There is a paradox that we are unable to resolve at this time. Recognizing the paradox helps move us closer to a solution for it, but the information or experience we need to resolve it is not yet available to us. The trick here is to avoid becoming bogged down by this. We need to get on with other aspects of our lives while acknowledging the difficulty here. If possible, we need to postpone related decisions and then relax about it, knowing that the insight we need *will* come—but we cannot rush it. In fact, trying to rush it usually only causes us to become more deeply mired in the confusion. Relax, wait, and stay alert.

"Faeries trip you up to give you a new perspective on the world."
—*Brian*

Card 61—G. Hobyah
Imaginary fears. Unreal hazards. Realistic caution.

He refuses to tell me what the *G* in his name stands for because, he says, the more we know about him, the less power he has and the harder it is to do his job. This tells you a lot about him. His powers lie in our imaginations and fears, not in the real world, not in *any* of the real worlds. This is the wicked thing in the closet who keeps frightened children awake at night with eerie snuffling, whuffling sounds—but when you turn on the light and open the door, he isn't there.

Brian wrote, "He exists only through the collection of our fears. The Hobyah thrives on fears, getting stronger and stronger until we face him. He is a sham—a tiny fear blown all out of proportion—and the smallest positive thought will banish him. All of Faeryland knows this and none is afraid of him."

G. Hobyah's job is to wave our imaginary fears in front of us, making them look as alive and real as he can. He's pretty good at this. The challenge he offers us is to see that certain fears of ours are imaginary and to distinguish them from things we actually need to be cautious about. In this way he tries to teach us to look past the fear and see real-i-o trul-i-o *truth*, whatever that truth is.

It is a difficult job, and G. Hobyah, the Pook, Gawtcha, the Fee Lion, and a few other hardworking faeries get together twice a week for otherworld nectar, hazelnuts, cheese, and apple sauce—and to grumble about humans and to support each other. The work they do, hard as it is, is merely an apprenticeship for the much harder work for which they get to wear a starry crown, like Epona's Wild Daughter (Card 54) and Lys of the Shadows (Card 44). It takes a *lot* of practice and skill in dealing with human flaws to get promoted to that level.

If you could hear the stories they tell . . .

Starter Reading It is time to look for the truth behind our fears, to distinguish between what is *real* and what is just our projection of old traumas and fears into our imaginary future. By delving into our old patterns, we can see past them to a more liberating life. Only by facing these fears honestly and

The Glanconer

seeing them for what they are do we gain greater ability to open our hearts to the Singer of Courage (Card 8) and gain in strength to face the *really* difficult challenges in our lives. Each false fear confronted and resolved makes us much stronger.

Reversed On the other hand, perhaps there *is* a wicked thing in the closet, waiting for the lights to be turned out. Check things out carefully—sometimes our fears are justified. It is important for us to learn to distinguish between the imaginary and the real.

Card 62—The Glanconer
Illusion. Delusion. Lust. Projection. Clear sight.

Have you ever noticed that when we really, really want someone or something, we tend to see it without clarity? The object of our lust looks flawless and glamourous, which should tell us something right away. But, usually, it doesn't.

He says his name is Smoothe Harry, but that may be a little illusion of his own. Unlike the Pook (Card 60), The Glanconer doesn't change his shape to tempt us with our own mental confusions and paradoxes. He simply wears a mirror in which we see our desires temptingly displayed. He doesn't try to fool us; he simply allows us to fool ourselves. Well . . . he may try just a *little*, just to make the test a little more difficult. After all, we can be more proud of passing a difficult test than an easy one, can't we?

Smoothe Harry also appeals to our vanity—and the more we have of it, the easier his work is. A little flattery and we'll believe whatever he wants us to swallow—especially since it is just what we want to swallow anyway. Of all the faery challengers, Smoothe Harry is the most likely to be sly. He practices a sort of emotional judo where he lets our own desires lead us into a fall. As we rush headlong toward our vision of perfection, he need only step to one side as we cast ourselves at him—and down we go. Not fun. But, maybe, perhaps, we might just learn something from it.

Starter Reading It is not good to make decisions when blinded by lust. Whether it is lust for a person, a thing, or an idea, we need to pause and take our time before making actual commitments. We need to read the fine print, check out the foundations, get a mechanic to test the so-beautiful secondhand car. If we are considering buying something, we can refuse to let ourselves be rushed into it and take time to make sure it is really what we think it is. If we are considering making a commitment to other people, we need to take our time and really get to know them much better. This is another lesson in seeing the truth behind a beglamoured surface, though in this case it is we who have cast the glamour.

Reversed Someone is pretending to be other than they really are. They may even believe (or at least want to believe) their own deceit, but probably not. This pretense may be because they want to please others, because they lack the moral strength to present themselves and their ideas honestly, or because they simply hope to gain an advantage by fooling others. Sometimes people fool themselves into thinking they are better than others and it is therefore all right for them to deceive. Although that is invalid logic, it is not uncommon. Vanity can be involved here, especially vanity based on something we know deep down to be untrue. False words like unmeant apologies may arise, or we may claim that something means little to us when, in fact, it means a great deal.

The others involved in the situation need to wake up and notice what is really happening instead of allowing themselves to be fooled. The situation needs to be handled with care, lest the awakening have very explosive, destructive effects.

If the pretender is the querent, she urgently needs to begin to present her true self and true ideas before things get much worse—as they certainly will, with the ensuing crises being even more devastating. This is the time to call upon Honesty (Card 40) for aid!

"Faeries are profound—profoundly annoying."
—*Brian*

63

Card 63—**Indi**

**Indecision. Wishy-washing.
Commitment. Decision making.**

If you don't get him on the wish, you
might catch him on the wash. But
probably not, because by the time you
think you've got a commitment from
him, he's swung the other way again.
Poor Indi, he can't decide between *this*
and *that*—or is it *that* and *this*? If he
just had more information, if he just
had some kind of guarantee about the
outcome, if only he could be *certain*
about things. Well, he can't. That isn't
how life is.

Indi sits on our shoulder as we
wobble around trying to make a decision, and just as we think we've about
got it, he mutters, "But, what if . . . ?"
And, very likely, we dissolve into confusion again.

Decisions make him nervous because they involve commitment,
and Indi seems to be frightened of that. What if he makes the wrong decision and it ruins his (or someone else's) life?

What if he makes no decision, dithering forever, and *that* causes
ruin?

I feel for Indi (and not only because I'm a Libra), for he is the only
one of the Faery Challengers who *doesn't* know what we should be doing.
That is, he knows we should be making our decisions clearly and cleanly at
the appropriate time, and he has some ideas about how we might more easily go about that, but he is not himself a good decision maker. Sometimes
he whispers almost tearfully in my ear, *"You're going to drive me mad, you know,
if you don't just* make . . . up . . . your . . . mind!"

There are many reasons why we hesitate when decision and action
are appropriate. However, most of them boil down to fear—fear of making
a mistake, fear of harming others, fear of losing something of value to us,
fear of harming ourselves, fear of responsibility, fear that we are simply not

able to make a proper decision. We need to look honestly at our insecurities, recognizing them for what they are: *our* insecurities, not reality. Then we need to resolve what we can and set the rest in the balance against what will surely happen if we continue to hesitate. Premature decisions and actions often create problems, but lack of decision is a decision also, and one that creates its own set of misfortunes.

Indi is also known as the Libra's Bane, but an indecisive Libra truly is Indi's bane. He would be so relieved if we would just make our decisions and our commitments and stick to them. Then he might learn to do this for himself and be in a better position to help others.

Caught up in Indi's energy, one Oracle group member who is usually a great decision maker herself responded to the above paragraph. "You lost me here. How would our learning to make decisions help Indi to make decisions? Would it really? Then what would he do? How would he better help other beings having problems with this? Or would the other beings that are having problems cause Indi not to learn to make his own decisions? Or are there no people that Indi knows that he can learn from now, so that he could be different? Or are we talking global change here???"

Er. What I was trying to say was that sometimes it is possible to learn from watching others learn. Indi would like to do this. Then he might be better able to teach those processes. Or perhaps not. At least, I *think* that is what I mean. The Unity (Card 1) knows there are plenty of beings who need help with this.

Starter Reading It's decision time. Time to make up your mind, make a decision, then stick to your commitments. Set yourself a definite time period to complete your decision, right down to the day and hour. Give yourself time to put the decision into practice before it is too late. Once that arbitrary but carefully judged decision time is set, ask for guidance for your highest good; then weigh, consider, ponder, and gather information. If we do this, and if we have asked for aid, the answer seems somehow to fall magically into place at the appointed time; then it is just a matter of trusting that answer and carrying it through. We can ask for help with that as well, if we wish. It is willingly given.

Reverse On the other hand, Indi may be right to hesitate. He may not have enough information to make an informed decision—and neither may you. Hesitate while you question. Find out more. True, we never will have

real guarantees from the universe about our decisions and their outcomes, but caution is appropriate here. Learn more. Get agreements in writing. If it doesn't feel right, maybe it *isn't* right. Consider well before you make promises about this—but once you do make the commitment, stick to it.

Card 64—Gawtcha

Sudden shock. Unexpected events. Rude awakenings.

Gawtcha is the Out of the Blue Faery. He likes to surprise us. You know—you're walking along, minding your own business (or not minding any business at all), and the universe smacks you on your blind side with something that makes an awful splat. Unexpected demands from the tax man. The bank's hole-in-the-wall machine eats your bank card late at night while the burly and irritable taxi driver is waiting. Your children find a way to dye themselves green just before your in-laws arrive. A meteor hits your car. Gawtcha is, of course, capable of happy surprises as well as shocking or miserable ones. Perhaps your lottery ticket wins.

There is a school of thought that says this is just karma—we deserve it for sins we have totally forgotten in other lifetimes. Not so. Karma is about lessons we need to learn, not about punishment; and meaningless events don't teach us much. So this may be karma, but it isn't *that* kind of karma.

There is another school of thought that says all of these things are our choices; we chose to be there when this was happening. We choose to step in front of the invisible cosmic bus. There is some truth to this—on one level of being high in the superconscious. As Gawtcha says, *"I know more than I see!"* But most of us don't function at that exalted intuitive level of consciousness much of the time. However, many of us *do* get hints, little flashes

> *"Bad faeries nip and prod us, asking for simple acknowledgment of their presence in our lives, insisting that we take notice of them—the first step to healing and change."*
> —Brian

of intuition, and sometimes even big flashes of intuition. We often say, "I *knew* I shouldn't have gone that way [or trusted that person, or invested in that stock]!"

There are two things Gawtcha is trying to teach us. (He says he doesn't enjoy doing it, but do I believe him? Actually, I do—mostly.) First, we need to learn to listen to and trust our intuition. We need to be awake and aware. It is just part of what we need to learn in order to fulfill our potential, to have happy and satisfying lives. Without it, we are sleepwalking in the world, missing all of the wonders and joys—while *not* missing many of the bumps and pitfalls.

Second, when there are lessons we need to learn or when there are experiences that are properly other people's but that have impact on us, we need to learn to roll with the punches, to take what comes at us, learn what we can from it, and regain our balance as quickly as possible. Things happen. We can't always control them, and we can't always get out of their way. We don't always even have a choice about them. For example, to live with a beloved animal friend probably means that you are going to lose that creature at some point, because most pets have shorter lifetimes than humans do. Other things happen as well. People occasionally win huge sums in lotteries, but this, too, we need to be able to take in our stride and not be completely lost in it.

Gawtcha knows we like to build sturdy, rigid structures in our minds and lives, but he also knows that these often are not good for us. Sometimes, we even complain about them, muttering about life being dull and boring—yet we cling to them tenaciously. Such inner and outer rigidities usually encourage stagnation, and the Unity (Card 1) insists on growth.

So, to help us along, Gawtcha kindly delivers these sudden surprises. Yet how often do we remember to say thank you? *"It's hard,"* Gawtcha says, *"doing such a difficult job. It's enough to drive a faery to drink."* From the look of that bloodshot eye, he has already been into some of the more potent otherworld nectar.

Starter Reading Gawtcha in a reading speaks to us of sudden, often violent, breakdowns of existing structures, habits, patterns, and/or attitudes. When we become too tightly confined by our own self-imposed limitations (including the desire for comfort and security), Gawtcha kindly breaks the structure restraining us—whether we think we want him to or not. On a soul level, we know this to be necessary, but in our everyday thoughts we usually get pretty upset about it. However, breakdown can lead to *break-through*. This is liberation—and we often haven't a clue what to do with it. This is usually the beginning of a period of confusion, even disorientation, while we search for a way forward—although we may think we are simply searching for a way back to what we had before.

Recommendation: Do *not* try to pick up the pieces and put them back like they were. Consider, instead, what you would like to build in that part of your life—and this time remember to leave room for growth.

Reverse Stagnation rules. It may seem that the situation is forever stuck, mired down in a swamp of misery, boredom, or pain. So it is—and it will remain so until someone, probably the querent, voluntarily sacrifices something outgrown but tightly clung to, in order to acquire something better. Bear in mind that the only truly meaningful sacrifice is ourselves—our time, our energy, our attitudes and beliefs. Gawtcha standing on his head suggests that we can break loose from this pattern by dedicating ourselves to some service, some voluntary but meaningful sacrifice that will loosen the knots, break loose the cement around the joints, and set us free. Gawtcha would like to see us do this and save him a lot of effort. *"Otherwise,"* he offers helpfully, *"I'll come and help you break loose just as soon as I have a moment to spare."*

Card 65—The Fee Lion
Getting it right. Delayed completions. Tidying up loose ends.

Brian notes that this is the accusing, offended expression we see on the cat's face, saying, "You *know* I have my dinner at five o'clock." Brian adds that the

Fee Lion is also known as a Slight Accusation or an Accusation of Slight. One of my cats, That Maggie, is the Fee Lion's first cousin, and has mastered the family expression. She uses it for all sorts of things, but I have often seen it elsewhere as well. I may even have used it myself, once or twice.

The Fee Lion

We know the Fee Lion is near, nodding his head, when we hear remarks like "I thought you'd have my shirt ironed for me," "You *said* you'd get the brakes fixed," or "You mean that report isn't done *yet?*"

The Fee Lion speaks to us when we know we deserve it but are pretending we don't. His is the voice that whispers in our ears just as we try to settle down with a good book, a new computer game, or our favorite leisure activities, and we experience that old, familiar guilty feeling. Alcohol only drowns him out temporarily and gives people hangovers as well, so it is not a useful remedy, although it is widely used. In fact, that particular avoidance tactic usually causes the Fee Lion to raise his voice even louder the next morning, in a particularly piercing tone.

He makes lists of things we haven't done, shaking his head over them and muttering, "*Tsk, tsk.*" These are the things we could and should have taken care of by now, but haven't. This is his job, and he does it well. Sometimes, though, he just wishes we would do our jobs so that he could go play First One over the Hill Gets to Kiss the Faery Maid or munch chocolate-covered thistles with his friends or take naps in the heather, instead of having to work overtime, nagging at us.

Starter Reading The Fee Lion looks out of his card accusingly, reminding us of things undone, promises unkept, and duties unfulfilled. He says that we can't expect to have things go right when we are trailing so much unfinished business behind us. Dragging that stuff around tires us; it uses up energy that we need for other things. If we would just take care of these things that cause so much mental (and sometimes physical) clutter, we would suddenly find that we have a lot more energy at our disposal to do the things that we really want to do—and probably much more cooperation from others as well. He especially suggests that we take care of the little things that matter to others. We will feel so much better when we have done that, and so will he.

Reversed The Fee Lion reversed says, *"Wait a minute! Whose idea was* this *anyway?"* He asks us to consider whose "oughts" and "shoulds" entangle us with feelings of guilt. Have we taken on a lot of unrealistic or unfair or plain silly demands from others? Are these old, irrelevant emotional programs we carry around from the past? The Fee Lion turned upside down suggests that we need to make a careful accounting of our guilty feelings and to decide just how many of them actually are our duty and how many are simply the result of other people making unfair or unrealistic demands of us—and we collude with this by acquiescing to such demands.

He also suggests that we take a look at how many of these unfinished tasks actually belong to others but have been taken on by us in a misguided attempt to be helpful or to appear obliging. Are we trying to make martyrs of ourselves? If so, it may well be that one part of us says (aloud, the foolish thing), "Oh, let me do that for you" while another part says silently (and mostly ignored), "It would be better all around if they did it for themselves." This sets up a conflict within us, and these conflicts use up a lot of energy, leaving us drained and unable to get on with our lives. These feelings can even be the cause of serious depression.

The way to resolve this one is either to do the job and then be smart enough not to make any more promises like that, or to give notice to the other people involved that we hereby hand them back their own responsibilities. This is hard stuff, but well worth the effort in present relief and future peace.

The Fee Lion would like to be our friend. He would like to read over our shoulders while we curl up with those good books. He'd like to dance in front of the computer screen while we play those new games or ride the golf balls we happily hit. *"Have you any idea of how much fun it is to ride a golf ball as it makes a hole in one?"* he asks. He can't do this until we can play with a clear conscience. The longer we put these duties off, the grumpier and more demanding and more shrill-voiced he gets. But when our tasks are done, he becomes a Free Lion, and no one is more magnificent than that.

I must go now; That Maggie says it's time for me to do my duty of tossing the catnip mouse for little cats to chase so that we all get some of our daily exercise—and this is the third time she's had to remind me already. Anyway, I've finished these "starter thoughts" for you now. I do hope they give you pleasure and other wonderful things!

"In Faery, secrets
are whispered
in the shape of a
wing or a faery's hue."
——Brian

"Faeries are seen not by the eyes but through the heart."
—Brian

Part Three
Going Deeper
Things you can have fun with and the faeries will enjoy helping you to learn

Preparing for a Reading

There are some simple things—meditation, earthing, centering, and connecting—that you can do to make yourself a better reader of any oracle. In addition to greatly improving our abilities as oracle readers, these things help us to more easily communicate with Faery and to lead lives that are more balanced and enjoyable. They are also all things that faeries enjoy doing with us.

Meditation

Meditation: Simple mental exercises in concentration that help you find the still, silent place within your being.

Meditation practice is essential to being an excellent oracle reader rather than a merely adequate one. If you meditate daily, you will find that your psychic and intuitive abilities gradually unfold like a flower in the sun. If you don't meditate, you can still learn to do these things, but the path is much longer and it is much more difficult to reach fluency and skill.

Here is a basic meditation exercise to try. Start by sitting comfortably but erect. Let your shoulders relax and your feet rest on the floor. Close your eyes. Be aware of your breath. Be aware of it coming in, going out. Be aware of how your body moves as you breathe. Imagine that you are breathing in through your navel and as you inhale, the breath rises to your throat. As you exhale, imagine your breath going back down and out through your navel. It's like a wave—in and up the shore, down and out to sea. Your breath will gradually and naturally change as you do this, becoming more relaxed and deeper. You don't need to do anything to make this happen; it just does. Let your breath move in its own time, at its own pace.

Alternatively, you might prefer this meditation instead. Sit comfortably but erect. Let your shoulders relax and your feet rest on the floor. Close your eyes. Choose a color that you feel will help to balance your energy at this moment. (This color is likely to vary on different days.) Use your intuition here and pick the color that *feels* right at this moment—don't just choose your favorite color. Visualize a circle of that color. Just keep looking at it. When it fades away or changes color or you get distracted, bring back the image of the color you started with. Don't get fancy with this; just keep it simple. You are practicing your ability to focus and keep your concentration so that when you read the Oracle cards you will be able to keep focused on the subtle messages of the cards rather than the noisy clamor that is usually in our minds.

Practice either exercise for ten minutes a day or find another that suits you better, as long as the focus is still on that one-pointed concentration of attention. You may also find it helpful to ask your Faery Guide to meditate with you; they are usually very good at it. It is often helpful to meditate with others, human or faery, especially if you are new to the practice. Once you begin finding this still point within, you will discover that it is the open gate to the many interesting things within yourself and in Faery.

In "Recommended Sources" at the back of the book there are resources listed where you can obtain much more information on meditation.

Contacting Planet Earth
Earthing (Grounding): **Connecting with the earth, exchanging your energy with hers, and allowing your energy to be cleansed and restored by her.**

Here is a grounding exercise called Using Your Tail to Stabilize Your Head. If you look at the pictures on the cards, you'll see that many faeries have tails. Actually, all of them do, though not all tails are visible. Humans also have tails made of subtle energy. Learning to be aware of yours and to use it not only helps you to be more grounded, but also helps you to become more aware of your own energy field and the interesting things you can do with it.

It's best to do this practice standing. Spread your feet about shoulder-width apart and balance on them so that your weight is distributed equally on the heels and the balls of your feet and your toes, and keep your knees slightly bent. Gently rock back and forth a bit until you feel balanced. (You many find that "balanced" is not where you usually stand, and you might want to think about that.)

Now, be aware of your breath. As you breathe in, imagine a gentle surge of energy running down from the top of your head to the tip of your tailbone. As you breathe out, imagine that energy moving through the spine back up to the top of your head. This is just your natural breath, neither hurried nor slow, but flowing in and out at whatever speed feels right at this moment. As you do this, the energy really *does* start moving gently up and down your spine. Just do it for a little bit. You may be able to feel something happen, but don't worry if you don't, because it *is* happening anyway. Be careful not to breathe too fast and hyperventilate. If you feel dizzy at all, consciously slow your breathing until the dizziness goes away.

(If this exercise makes you uncomfortable in some way, try just imagining the energy moving in your spine from the top of your head to behind your heart. Then each day, as you feel ready to do so, let it go a little farther down. *Do not* push it; that usually only causes problems. Just let it develop and deepen at its own pace.)

After you have let the energy move up and down your spine a few times, start letting it go *below* your tailbone into your energy tail as you inhale. Each time let it go a little lower, until it touches the floor. Then let it go deeper still until it touches the earth. Each time you exhale be aware of the energy rising to the top of your head.

Then let it go deeper still, until it goes several inches *into* the earth beneath you. Just practice doing this for a while, going into the earth and back to the top of your head with this small energy. Don't push it; just let it happen. This not only earths your energy, it also cleanses and brightens up your entire subtle energy field. Being earthed is what helps us to be realistic and practical, down-to-earth on the physical level of being as well as the energetic and mental. When we are earthed, we are also less easily confused by the energy and thoughts of other people.

If you want to you can let it go even deeper. If you don't feel ready to do that at first, don't. Just let it go deeper when you feel ready to do so. This whole exercise needs to be done at a gentle pace, never pushing, just relaxing into the natural movement of the energy. This line of energy is already there, a part of your being. What you are really developing is awareness and control of it.

For the last breath of your practice, think of the energy rising from the earth, up through your spine, and breathe it out of your mouth in a puff. Then bend over a bit, letting your arms hang loose, and wiggle your shoulders. Stand back up slowly. Can you still feel your tail? If you find later on that you can't still sense it, just do a few energy-moving breaths to get your awareness of it refocused.

Hopefully, you are earthed through your feet as well as your tail. (You can use this same exercise to run energy through your legs as well.) If so, you can lift your tail and do things with it, like touching a flower to explore its energy or gently stroking the cat. Don't try to play tricks on people or intrude on them with your energy tail or the universe will teach you why such behavior is inappropriate. *Those* lessons are usually not fun, so be careful what you stick your tail into. However, developing strength, flexibility, and awareness in your energy field is a lot of fun, so . . . enjoy!

With practice, any earthing exercise becomes easier to do and takes effect more quickly. Getting practiced at it means that we have a wonderful tool for those stressful moments when Ffaff the Ffooter (Card 58) lifts our feet into the air and leaves them there.

Centering
Centering: Being focused in your own being, balanced within and moving in the world like a surfer well balanced on a wave.

To be centered is to be balanced in your own being, looking out at the world from your own personal inner position of power. When we are not centered in ourselves, we are usually centered in something or someone else—an idea, an emotion, a possession, another person's ideas, emotions, or desires.

Being centered, if we are not naturally good at it, may require a lot of practice. Here is an easy exercise to try (at least compared with learning to be a good surfer). Begin by sitting with your feet flat on the floor (or better yet, on Earth herself, if convenient). Imagine that you are inhaling through your navel, letting the breath rise to your throat, and then exhaling through your navel (as in the first meditation exercise). After a couple of minutes, begin to imagine that you are inhaling through the soles of your feet, letting the breath rise through your pelvis, abdomen, and heart, and then letting it fall again, exhaling through the soles of your feet. Gradually let the incoming breath rise to the top of your head, still being aware of it passing through your pelvis, abdomen, and heart as it travels each way. Breathe gently and naturally into and from the earth until you feel calm and peaceful.

When we are centered, we know how we *really* feel about things, and we have a much clearer sense of what is appropriate and inappropriate for us. Sometimes, we don't like how we feel, and that is when we are tempted to become uncentered by denying our feelings. It is much more helpful in the long run to acknowledge our feelings and *do* something about the situation, the issue, and/or our own attitudes. There is always a faery who is willing to help us with this, if we ask.

Connecting
Connecting: creating rapport with our higher selves, faeries, and the powers that be—whomever you relate to in the higher realms. This allows us to intuitively access the wisdom of Faery, the Faeries' Oracle, and other sources of wisdom.

For connecting, each of us must discover our own best path. However, I can tell you what I do, and that might give you some ideas about what will work for you. For the most part I use both imagery and prayer in order to connect. I thank my source of guidance for the aid that I've received in the past, and I request help in what I am about to do and in finding the best guidance for all concerned. To this, I add a mental image of the energy of the upper realms showering down onto and into me. I let it flow through my feet into Earth, knowing that I am receiving what I need and feeling gratitude for it.

This is simple. Sometimes people feel like it needs to be really complex and elaborate, but that is not necessary. A long rote prayer is often far less effective than a few brief words that are truly felt in the heart. Take time to focus on the *feeling* of connection, of being cherished, of being open to love and wisdom, and of gratitude for that guidance. That feeling is the real connection; any words we use are just there to help us find it.

Just as there are two ways of connecting with the earth—through our feet and through our energy tails—there are two ways of connecting with our sources of guidance, the faeries: through our minds and through our hearts. The description of connecting above is primarily through our minds, but it is also important to connect to our source of guidance through our hearts, if we wish to read for ourselves or others with both compassion and wisdom.

A way of connecting through the heart is to use our wings. Faeries have wings, but do you realize that you have them, too? They are part of the human energy structure, just as our tails are. This tells us that we are more like the faeries than many people suppose. Our wings open and close in response to how we are feeling. Have you ever consciously tried to spread your wings out? They are naturally spreadable to the extent that our hearts are open—and spreading them out *helps* our hearts to open more widely. I am being literal here, not metaphorical. We have real wings, made up of the same stuff as our energy bodies. Often, we keep them furled at our backs, perhaps afraid of hurting them—but they don't hurt easily and they can heal rapidly if we help the process by opening them.

So, how do we unfold them? Pretty simple, really.

Sit or stand quietly somewhere so that your back is free and there is plenty of room behind you. Shut your eyes. Let yourself relax. Be aware for a few moments of the energy in the center of your chest as it pulsing with your heart. Be aware next of where the energy flows *into* the heart from the back. If you go "upstream" along that flow of energy, it reaches into two cushionlike energy structures behind your back, which gather in energy from the universe. You may be able to sense these right away, or you may not be able to do so without quite a bit of practice. If you can't feel them at first, just imagine them being there—they work either way.

These energy structures are like furled flowers—or wings. You can open them. Just imagine them opening like flowers in the sun, softly, gently, one feather-petal at a time. The "sun" they open to is the compassionate, loving wisdom flowing through the cosmos. It is just there; we only need to open ourselves to it. The more you relax into this, the less you *try* and the more you just allow it to happen, the better it works. It feels much like a whole-body smile.

See how widely your wings want to stretch out at this moment. You may find yourself involuntarily smiling as you do this—that's fine; it's just another sign that the wings are spreading out. They are a kind of energy antenna gathering in loving wisdom—and joy as well.

These wings absorb subtle, loving, and healing energies from the cosmos around us along with wisdom. Consciously opening our wings lets them absorb more. This energy, both physical and subtle energy, flows into our hearts and helps to heal and regenerate us physically and emotionally. It then naturally flows onward, through our hearts, to those we love and those we wish to serve. If our wings are open as we read the cards and connect with faeries, much more of their compassionate wisdom comes through the reading.

In addition to the card readings, at other times you can, of course, do intentional things with these wings—healing, loving, comforting yourself and others. Be careful of your ethics here, making sure others want this from you before you do it. Don't just push it at them or you might get your wings bruised as they push you back, and rightly so. This energy that flows through our wings into our hearts and, if we wish, on through to others is unlimited. It belongs to all of us and there is plenty of it—far more than we could ever begin to use. It is available everywhere; we only need to avail ourselves of it. And to *remember* to keep our wings spread widely.

You can do all sorts of things with these wings. Like the Singers' wings, yours can reach across all of space and time. It does take some practice (!) to reach that point. Just watch your wings and see when they naturally open up. Notice how they begin to close when you become tense or worried. Be gentle with yourself when you notice that you have closed your wings, and gently reopen them. Soon you will find yourself open more of the time, just naturally. It is especially helpful to remember to spread them in the acts of prayer, spiritual healing, and oracle reading.

So, what we have seen in this chapter is that **meditation** helps us to find the silence in our minds, where we can truly listen to the faeries and other spiritual guidance. **Earthing** (grounding) helps us to be practical and down-to-earth—even about esoteric beings like faeries and activities like the reading of oracles. Being **centered** enables us to recognize what is truly appropriate for us when we hear it—and to recognize what isn't right for us. Being **connected** allows us access to the wisdom of Faery, both through our minds and our hearts. When we are earthed, centered, connected, and in a calm, meditative state we are fully part of the wholeness of all being. In that place, miracles sometimes happen. In fact, they happen quite often, I find.

"To engage with Faery, stay open and let the faeries speak to you. Let them enfold you in faery light. If you desire an emotional or physical healing, direct that thought through the imagery to the light energy of the faery realm. Remember, as each man and woman is a microcosm reflecting the larger natural world, so healing of the self is also a healing for the world. As above, so below."

—Brian

Reading the Oracle for Others

As you read the cards of *The Faeries' Oracle*, a time will quickly come when you will probably want to read for others as well as yourself. A friend or member of your family might ask what you are doing with those cards and, well . . . it is easier to simply show them than to explain. In fact, many of you probably already do read cards for others, but to some of you it may be new. Reading for others is much like reading for yourself, with just a few extra things to add. The following notes follow the same basic pattern for readings that we went through in "Reading the Cards," but I've added explanations of extra things we do when reading for others.

1. **Request aid and guidance from the faeries in doing the reading.**
2. **Attune yourself to the cards and the querent (the person for whom you are reading) and who is asking the question.**

Attuning: connecting with the querent so that you are energetically in harmony with him. Each of us has to find our own best way to do this. What I do is to hold the hands of the querent, asking him to close his eyes. Then I do a brief *silent* earthing exercise, *silently* inviting them to join me in it. Doing this aloud often just produces confusion and the need for long explanations. It seems to work better silently. Then I say something like the following prayer: Please help me to understand and give the information this person most needs at this time for his greatest and highest good. Please help me to put this information in the terms that he will best understand. May we be guided together to truth, insight, wisdom, and the path to joy.

Then I release his hands and we go on to the next step, defining the question, which usually helps to deepen the attunement.

3. **Define the question to be addressed in the reading.**

This is just the same except that you help the querent to define his question clearly. Two heads are better than one for this.

4. **Shuffle the cards, if desired, while focusing on the question.**

This is also the same as in "Reading the Cards" except that you may have the querent shuffle the cards instead of doing it yourself. I prefer to have the querent shuffle them, and then I spread the cards in front of the querent in an arc, as described earlier. I like for the querent to participate as much as possible in the process of setting up the cards.

5. **Choose the cards, placing them facedown on the work surface.**

How the cards are chosen is up to you as the reader. You can deal them off the top of the deck or you can choose them from the arc of cards you have made in front of the querent. Either you or the querent can choose the cards. Again, this is something I prefer the querent to do himself,

6. One by one, turn the cards over, acknowledging the presence of the faery shown on the card and asking them what they wish to tell the querent.

Begin with Card One of the layout. You can turn the cards over or you can ask the querent to do so, but in either case *decide in advance* whether you or the querent are going to flip the cards end for end or turn them over sideways.

You also need to decide in advance who is the center of the reading—the querent or you. Are the cards right side up if they are right side up to you or if they are right side up to the querent? I prefer to work with the cards relative to the querent rather than to myself. I call the kind of readings I do "querent-centered" and querents have an active involvement in them. They handle and help shuffle the cards, they choose the cards, they usually create the layout (see "Faery-Style Readings"), they turn the cards faceup when it is time, and we tend to discuss things as we go. I want them to understand that they are participating in the process, and that it is about *their* making informed choices to co-create their future with the universe. I see myself as a facilitator in the querent's magical process rather than as the director of it. This is neither the "right" nor the "wrong" way to work—it is just *my* way and it works well for me. Experiment and find the way that is right because it works for you.

7. Tell the querent the faery messages, as appropriate, and discuss how the messages relate to the position of the card in the layout, if you are using more than one card.

This is much the same as reading for yourself, except that you describe the images and impressions that come to you to the querent as you go.

Remember to just trust the process as you describe the feelings and ideas that come to you as you look at the cards. As you get better at working with the free-flowing energy/information of the faeries, you will find that the querent more and more often interrupts you to say, "It's so weird that you should say that because . . ." and forms some wonderful connection between the faery message and what is going on in her life.

In addition, of course, you can explain to the querent who the faery is, what the faery's special field of interest is, and how that might apply to the issue at hand. Again, the querent will often form her own connections.

You don't have to have all the answers; in fact, you probably *can't* have all the answers, and it is better that you don't.

Here is the Magical Macbeth Theory of Reading and Counseling: *On some level, every person knows what her problem really is. And she knows, on some level, exactly what she needs to do about it. The reader / counselor's job is to help ask the questions and provide the clues that will enable that person to access that information in the way that is most clear and most meaningful to her.*

Isn't that marvelous? Not only do you not have to know everything, but the process usually works much better for querents if you don't, and if they discover answers for themselves.

When you get stuck in this reading process, which happens even to experienced readers, just pause and close your eyes. (If you can put an intelligent, listening expression on your face while you do this, the querent tends to assume that wonderful things are happening outside of her ken.) Breathe. Earth. Center. Connect. Remember what it felt like when you were dancing and singing with the faeries. When you feel centered and connected, open your eyes and look at the card again. Don't rush. Don't try to fill up the silences with words, just to be talking. Use the silences to listen and go on from there.

8. Get feedback from the querent, and work with any additional and related questions he may have.

While you are learning to read oracles, verification of information obtained psychically is very important. Some things, of course, can't be verified because the querent doesn't know about them yet, but welcome feedback from him as you do the reading.

It is through such practical experience that we learn to distinguish between psychic information and the unconscious contents of our own minds. You will find with experience that psychic information has a characteristic feeling. Sometimes there are physical signals—itches, twitches, tickles, or other sensations—or perhaps just a sense of energy somewhere in your body. These signals are ephemeral; they happen for a while and then change, but they do tell us that something magical is going on deeper in consciousness. They give us verification of connection with Faery, a kind of feedback from our own bodies and energy fields.

Honest and intelligent feedback from other people is also extremely helpful in developing the ability to recognize psychic information for what it is. If you are practicing with someone else as you learn—and I strongly recommend that you do—honesty in feedback is vital. It is as bad to tell someone that they are correct when wrong or that you understand the information when you do not as it is to deny the validity of something you know to be true. Please note that there is a difference between information you don't understand and information you know to be incorrect. This distinction should be made when giving feedback.

Also, it is helpful to realize that when someone says, "I don't know" or "I don't understand," they are not saying you are wrong. Feedback is a tricky business. Sometimes the querent doesn't know about something, sometimes he doesn't want to talk about it, and sometimes he is in denial about it. All we can really do, as readers, is the best we can to work our way through this maze.

9. Summarize the story or theme of the reading for the querent.

Summarize the reading as you have learned to do for yourself in "Reading the Cards." You might want to ask the querent a couple of questions before you finish, just to be certain that she has the message clear. For you, the reader, this is a little check to see that the querent has understood what you said.

10. Close down the reading and clear the connection with the querent.

Develop you own ritual for ending the reading. This needs to include earthing, centering, and connecting. It also needs to include letting go of the reading. Again, each of us has to find what works best for ourselves, but those elements need to be a part of it. What I do is to make certain we are finished with the reading and then gather up the cards. As I shuffle them and put them back into a neat pile, I thank the querent for sharing and bless him. Then, I set the cards down between us, mentally releasing the person and the reading as I let go of the cards. Then I change the subject or see him out the door, whichever is appropriate. Whenever possible, I avoid continuing to discuss the reading with the querent at that time because that usually only leads to a muddle.

As discussed in "Reading the Cards," this is the time when you are moving back into ordinary consciousness from the special focused mental state of the reading. This is a good time to go and fix something refreshing for both of you to eat or drink, just to give yourself a break before you try to interact with others in a more ordinary way.

11. Thank those who have helped you.

12. Earth, center, connect, and release any attachments to outcomes for the reading.

While you are giving yourself a break from the querent, again earth, center, and connect. Ask that the energy flowing through you clears and strengthens your own energy. I also find it very helpful, both for myself and the querent, to say a silent little prayer asking that the querent be guided and helped in whatever ways are appropriate. Then I turn the whole thing over to the querent's faery helpers and his own higher self, and I go on about my business.

All done!

These are the main things you need to know about reading the Faeries' Oracle for others. As you do these readings you will find that each one—whether for yourself or others—teaches you something that enhances your own life and your connection with Faery and all of its delights, as well as providing an avenue of joyful and fulfilling service to others. In the next chapter we'll find more detailed information about card layouts and faery-style reading.

"I believe in the artist as shaman, journeying deep into uncharted inner worlds, then bringing back sensations and visions encountered in that mythic terrain.

"I see my pictures as maps of the journeys I've taken through the realms of the soul. And I hope that these maps will lead you to find faery pathways of your own."
—Brian

Faery-Style Readings

Faery-style oracle readings are a free-form, free-flowing process in which the question and the energy of the reading itself dictate the card spread and the flow of the reading. They are often more accurate and revealing than following a card-spread formula, in part because they are absolutely attuned to the needs of the moment. Doing these faery-style readings is easier than you may expect—and you won't have to memorize all those card spreads.

Although this chapter describes the reading as if you were reading for other people, you can, of course, do the same type of readings for yourself. I hope you will enjoy them both ways.

Faery Readings

Meditate. Earth and center. Connect. Ask the faeries for assistance with the reading. Attune to the querent. Define the question clearly.

Ask the querent to choose a number between one and nine. That will be the number of cards you use in the reading. (You can make the options more than nine, if you like, but I recommend keeping the numbers low when you are first learning this technique.) This whole process is very intuitive, and the querent choosing the number of cards is where the intuition starts.

Next, arc the cards facedown in front of him, and have him pick out and place the number he has chosen on the open space in front of him. Suggest that he take his time choosing the cards and look for the ones that seem to "call" to his eyes or to his fingers. The cards are not to be placed in any special order. The querent is to be instructed to put each card, facedown, wherever it *feels right* to put it. As he is doing this, notice where he puts the cards he chooses first, and also notice which cards he chooses quickly and which he hesitates over.

Quickly chosen cards may (but do not always) indicate something the querent already knows or almost knows, or something that is readily acceptable to him. Cards that are hesitated over can indicate resistance or information that isn't very definite yet—or other things. These are just possible indications and not absolutes, and you as the reader must go with your own intuition on this. Quickness or hesitation can also just be the querent's personal style, so what you are looking for is something out of the ordinary *for that person*. It is usually best not to say anything about these hesitations to the querent, especially at this point, as that only makes him self-conscious, but it may be useful to you as you go along with the reading.

Now, the intuition of the reader comes into play. Again, check to be sure you are earthed, centered, and connected. Let yourself move into the tranquil, meditative state in which we do our best reading. Take your time to get that right. Now, look at the facedown cards and work out what the pattern is. For example, let's assume that the number chosen is five and the question is "What can I do to improve my performance at work?" Then the querent lays out the cards like this:

Just look at the backs of the cards and ask the faeries to guide you in defining the layout. Here is where you *just make things up* and trust the energy of the reading and of Faery to guide you appropriately. You might be looking at the backs of the cards and find yourself thinking that Card

"Faeries dwell in the twilight, between day and night, between spirit and matter, between the conscious and the unconscious ... where all things are possible, where the past and the future meet, where we meet ourselves coming back.

"When we dance with the faeries, we dance with the reflections of our true selves and the true inner self of the world."
—Brian

number Two here looks like a block or an obstacle. Go with that idea and then ask yourself what Card One is likely to be. Well, perhaps it *feels like* it talks about the situation the querent is in now, facing that block. Go with that. It may be just a feeling or a hunch, but that is exactly what we are working with. Then look at the two angled cards, Three and Four. They feel to me like two different things the querent might do to improve his performance. In this particular layout at this moment Card Five *feels* to me like the goal and what he will get by achieving it. So there you have the definition of the layout. *This* layout, for *this* moment, is as follows:

1. Where the person is now with respect to performance on the job
2. The main obstacle in his way to improvement
3. Something he can do to improve
4. Something else he can do to improve
5. The goal—what difference the improvement in cards Three and Four will make and how that will affect his work

Then, you just treat it like any other defined layout (like the three-card versions in "Basic Card Spreads") and read each card according to its position. This works very well, but if you try to second-guess the placement of the cards in the layout after you've already turned the cards over, it is almost always very confusing. Just trust the process, define the layout from the back, and then read the cards one by one within the framework of that layout.

Another example: Suppose someone chooses the number four and asks, "What do I need to do to improve my relationship with my friend Suzy?" Then, suppose she lays out the cards in a "stair" like this:

This layout could very well indicate that the reading shows a straightforward process, one step after another in an orderly and timely manner. The only tricky bit is in intuitively determining where she now is in the process. Which is the *now* card? You could ask yourself this and then wait to see which card "pulls" at your eyes, because it has the *now* energy. Or you might move one hand across and above the cards and see which one "pulls" at your hand. Remember, these are often very subtle feelings at first, and only become clearer with practice. Trust even the most subtle feeling, the faintest warmth or tickle or tingle, go with the energy of it, and that will get you there. If it isn't clear fairly quickly, pause, breathe, earth, center, connect, and try again. If it *still* isn't clear, try moving your hand or eyes to the space *before* the "lowest" card on the stair because the *now* energy in that space would indicate that the first step shown by the cards is yet to be taken. The calmer and more centered you are and the more you trust your *first* impulse, the first subtle signal, the better it works.

Let's try one more reading, and this time include the interpretation of the cards. This time I shall ask a question for myself. Number of cards, five. Question: How can I improve my ability to read the Faeries' Oracle? Then I lay the cards out like this:

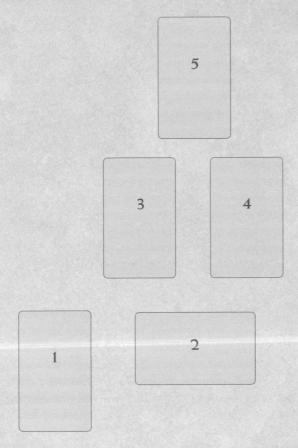

Looking at the backs of the cards, the definition of the layout that comes to my mind is (One) what helps me now, (Two) what hinders me now, (Three and Four) how I can break through this hindrance, and (Five) where this takes me.

As I turn the cards over one by one, I find that the first one is He of the Fiery Sword (Card 4). I take this to mean that what helps me is my ability to take action and trust in the process. However, the second card in the layout, The Singer of Connection (Card 6), suggests that I am not as well connected as I could be—I need to work more on being better earthed, better centered, and especially better connected—remembering to *ask* the faeries and the Singers for help when I have a problem.

The third and fourth cards make me rethink the second card a bit. The Topsie-Turvets (Card 51) is the third, and it suggests to me that I need to look at this in a different way, a way that I haven't thought of before. Spirit Dancer (Card 36) in the fourth position tells me that creative expression is important. I think I am being mildly scolded here. I've been working so hard on this book that I haven't taken time to play and sing and dance with the faeries, and I've not sculpted anything or taken time out for my garden. I've been in my thinking-head mode instead of my joyful-creative mode. If I want to read the cards well, which I *must* do for Part Two, I need to refocus myself more into that faery-communication space of creative and joyful expression. Though I may feel pressed to hurry, hurry, hurry and get this done, it can only be done well if I stay centered joyfully and playfully in the moment—so that is what I must do.

The fifth card in the layout is the Singer of Courage (Card 8). Ah, this card reminds me that there is a nervous part of me that wonders, "But can I do this well enough? What if I let Brian and Faery down by *not getting it right?*" My old and often-conquered inner program about having to do things perfectly rears its ugly little head again. When I am in thinking-head mode, things like this worry me. When I am in joyful-creative mode, they don't; *then* I trust the process, trust the faeries to guide me, and trust that they and Brian have chosen me rightly and that it will all be fine. And fun. And I just need to do it.

It's funny, isn't it, how much courage depends on trust? I've had this message before—it seems to be a lifetime project for me—but I'm not surprised to get it again at this moment. The Singer of Courage was reversed, and I take that to mean that this is an ongoing lesson that is not likely to be completed immediately. To check that interpretation, I draw a companion card and get Geeeeeooo the Slooow (Card 43), so I understand that I have to just keep plugging away at it. There is much more to the reading than just this and it runs more deeply, but this is enough for you to see how this kind of reading works.

Of course, when we finish a reading, we do all the closing down steps described in "Reading the Cards." In that respect, these readings are like any others.

The really weird, wild, and wonderful thing about this is that whatever definition of the layout we choose, it always seems to work. The querents get information they need. The faeries tell us what needs to be known. It is, in fact, quite magical. And so is the next way of reading the Faeries' Oracle.

Faery Counseling

When we sit down with a person to read an oracle, there are different approaches we can take. One choice is simply to give the message first seen in the cards. This doesn't require feedback from or interaction with the querent. This also tends to assume that the reader's interpretation is infallible and the future is fixed. The problem with this, of course, is that things are not fated. The querent has free will and so does everyone else. The best we can do about predicting the future is to read a *potential* future, which is the thing most likely to happen if everyone behaves as they typically act—and if no one chooses to exercise their free will or their free won't.

Another approach is to read the cards like the first method, but to make it clear that any information about the future is only a probability, not something fated to happen. One could even suggest that if the querent doesn't wish this outcome, he could attempt to take steps to change it.

The third approach (and the one that I much prefer) is to treat the reading as an interaction with the querent, one in which you, the reader, can also ask questions and the querent can give you feedback as you go. For example, you can ask the querent what a particular card or a particular symbol means to her and incorporate that information into the reading. There are no faery laws (or human, either) saying that the querent can't give valuable input into the reading—and in fact, her contribution may be the most valuable of all.

"Remember, each journey into Faery is complete only when we come home again and make human sense of faery nonsense, passing on or making use of whatever we have learned."
—Brian

If you are reading for yourself this can be one of the challenging parts of playing the roles of both reader and querent. It requires a delicate balance to maintain, on the one hand, the meditative state and objectivity of a good reader, while on the other hand examining your own feelings and responses to what is coming up in the reading. It can be done but it takes practice. In reading for myself I find that talking out loud helps. I tell myself what I see or sense about the cards, and then I reply just as I would to another reader. Maintaining that essential meditative state while reading can be done if we are clear about when we are reading and when we are letting ourselves respond to the reading. Of course, switching roles back and forth this way is also good practice in being more observant and insightful about ourselves.

There are other possibilities to consider in readings as well. For example, if a faery card for the future comes up with a prediction that the querent doesn't like, you can ask her how she *wants* the situation to come out instead. Then you can ask the faeries to guide you, through the cards, to an understanding of what the querent needs to change in herself or in her situation in order to achieve her goals as much as possible. Then you may draw another card (or more than one) to get that guidance. You might even stop reading the first card spread altogether and do a second one focused on how she might create positive change in the situation.

Obviously, you have to take into consideration that not everything is within the power of the querent to change. Some things depend on the choices and actions of others. However, even then the querent can discover ways of seeing and coping with the situation that may be much more productive and satisfying than her old, habitual ways. Here we are moving from the realm of *reading* into the realm of *counseling*.

Counseling is a mutually supportive activity in which the counselor helps the seeker to clarify his true goals and find the most productive paths toward them. In this process, the seeker also learns new ways of approaching his problems. Instead of becoming increasingly dependent on the counselor for advice and support, the querent learns more effective ways of solving his own difficulties. This provides less ego gratification for the reader, but it is much more empowering for and helpful to the querent.

This style of reading is very free flowing and adaptable to the needs of the moment. It also gives the reader the joy of being involved in the creation of a more insightful, wiser, and more joyful future for the querent. And chances are, you will also learn something from the faeries and something from the querent that will help you improve the levels of insight, wisdom, and joy levels in your own life, making the co-creative process full of wonders all around.

You get to choose which way you want to work. May each reading you do, for yourself or others, be filled with faery wisdom and faery joy!

We can invite the faeries to play with us in a way that is healing for all of us. Almost always, they love to do that and are pleased to be asked, and then it is easy to bring healing energy into an Oracle reading.

When we are earthed, centered, and connected and allowing the energy of Faery to flow through us in reading its Oracle, healing just naturally happens. It can be that simple. We can facilitate our openness to this by asking in our opening statement of intent that both the reading and we ourselves be a channel for healing.

There are a few things we can do to facilitate the flow of healing energy: stay in a meditative, calm state as we read; keep our posture erect, balanced, and open so that we don't block or scrunch up the energy as it goes through us; keep our hearts open to the querent and to Faery; and keep our emotional balance so that we don't find ourselves trying to please the querent rather than trying to tell her what she needs to hear—truth, kindly and lovingly expressed, which in itself is very healing.

Then, all that is needed is receptivity on the part of the querent. Healing takes place on various levels—body, mind, emotions, and soul. Just because we don't see them doesn't mean that miracles are not happening.

It's quite straightforward, really. And when these unexpected miracles of healing take place, it is faery wonderful for all of us, readers, querents, and faeries alike.

The Faeries' Oracle is a gateway, an open invitation to explore Faery, the human psyche, and beyond. Enjoy!

> *"Listen to the voice of*
> *the wind in the trees;*
> *it has a message for you."*
> —*Brian*

Recommended Sources

If you are on the Internet

If you are on the Internet, there are several ways you can participate in the Faeries Oracle and Froudian activities.

First, there is The World of Froud, Brian and Wendy Froud's official Web site, at:

http://www.worldoffroud.com.

At that Web site you can join the announcement list that will keep you updated on Brian and Wendy Froud's tours, new books, art exhibitions, and other activities, and link to discussion groups for *The Faeries' Oracle*. You can even send a faery card to your friends from there.

My Web site, Jesa Macbeth's Coracle, is at:

http://www.pobox.com/~jesamac.

I also facilitate several e-mail discussion lists. Subscriptions are free. To subscribe to any of them, send a blank e-mail to the following addresses:

FaeryOracle-subscribe@eGroups.com (This list is for people to discuss the Oracle and the world of Faery, sharing their skills and learning from each other.)

oas-subscribe@eGroups.com (This is a more general discussion list, mainly on the topics of healing, meditation, and related subjects.)

There is also a very basic beginning meditation course up on my Web site:

http://www.pobox.com/~jesamac/meditate.html

We invite you to join us at any of these places.

Recommended Books

First, of course, if you haven't already read it, is *Good Faeries / Bad Faeries* by Brian Froud. There you will encounter, through Brian's vision and words, many of the faeries in *The Faeries' Oracle* plus many of the faeries who are not visible in the *Oracle* but who are nevertheless really there. Brian's thoughts and experiences with these faeries will give you much valuable insight into *The Faeries' Oracle* itself (Simon & Schuster, 1998).

Moon Over Water by Jessica Macbeth tells you what you really need to know about meditation, earthing, and centering (Gateway Books, 1990).

Sun Over Mountain by Jessica Macbeth gives clear information on working with guided imagery to enhance contact with the faeries and to facilitate other personal and spiritual processes (Gateway Books, 1991).

Complete Book of Tarot Spreads by Evelin Burger and Johannes Fiebig has 122 card spreads and interesting exercises that would work well with *The Faeries' Oracle* (Sterling Publishing Co., 1997).

James Wanless's *Strategic Intuition for the 21st Century: Tarot for Business* shows how to incorporate tarot into everyday life, especially in making business decisions (Merrill-West Publishing, 1997).

Steps to a Good Reading

Note: "Querent" refers to you if you are reading for yourself or to another person if you are reading for them. It simply means the person who is asking the questions on which the reading is based.

1. Meditate, earth, center, and connect.
2. Request aid and guidance from the faeries in doing the reading.
3. Attune yourself to the querent (this is really easy if the querent is yourself).
4. Define the question to be addressed in the reading.
5. Shuffle the cards, if desired, while mentally focusing on the question.
6. Choose the cards, placing them face down on the work surface.
7. One by one turn the cards over, acknowledging the presence of the faeries shown on the card and asking them what they wish to tell you.
8. Tell the querent the faery messages, as appropriate, and if you are using more than one card, discuss how the messages relate to the position of the card in the layout.
9. Get feedback from the querent and work with any additional and related questions.
10. Summarize the story or theme of the reading for the querent.
11. Close down the reading; if you are reading for someone else, clear the connection with the querent.
12. Thank those who have helped you.
13. Earth, center, connect, and release any attachments to outcomes for the reading.

About the Authors

BRIAN FROUD is an artist and author who has created such bestselling books as *Good Faeries / Bad Faeries*, *Strange Stains and Mysterious Smells*, *Lady Cottington's Pressed Fairy Book*, and *Faeries*. The conceptual designer for Jim Henson's films *The Dark Crystal* and *Labyrinth*, he lives in Devon, England, with his wife, Wendy, and their son, Toby.

JESSICA MACBETH is the author of *Moon Over Water* and *Sun Over Mountain*, two guides to meditation and self-discovery. She has taught faery communication and other metaphysical subjects for over thirty years. She lives in Port Townsend, Washington, and Scotland.

Notes

Notes

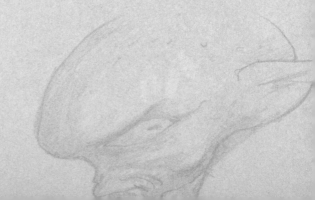